CONTINENTAL DESSERT
DELICACIES

CONTINENTAL DESSERT DELICACIES

BY ALICE SIDON

M. BARROWS & COMPANY

Incorporated

NEW YORK

In memory of my dear friend Ruth Klein in whose home the idea of this book was conceived.

THIS BOOK is created for the many Americans who have visited Continental Europe and enjoyed the unusual dessert delicacies of those countries, or for those who have relished the tortes, strudels, crèmes and such sweets offered in "foreign" restaurants and bakeries here.

The author collected these recipes while living in Europe and has employed them so successfully in her home that now she has translated them for all to use. Dessert-loving gourmets will be especially pleased to find such culinary know-how in one book.

The recipes are not designed for the young bride who dashes into her kitchen at five o'clock to create a heavenly treat for her new husband to eat at seven. They are to be taken much more seriously for, like most traditionally fine foods, they were evolved when speed was not an important consideration and when eggs, cream and other expensive ingredients were used lavishly—and justifiably—to produce perfection. Most of them are definitely party-fare and, because of their richness, should be served in small portions, perhaps with strong black coffee.

RUTH P. CASA-EMELLOS
Home Economist
The New York *Times*

CONTENTS

~~~~~~

The importance of the dessert in a well-planned menu cannot be sufficiently stressed. Though psychologists claim that first impressions are the lasting ones, their conclusion can hardly apply to the pleasures of the palate where the savor of the last course—the dessert—lingers on. Should anything go amiss with a previous course, a good dessert becomes the *pièce de résistance* that saves the party.

This book of recipes has been prepared at the urgent request of friends who have found my desserts so different from the usual run of today's ready-mix cakes, puddings and gelatins, useful as they are. Each of my recipes is European in origin and all have been accumulated before my arrival in the United States. Some have been acquired from cooks who have been in the employ of my family. One of these was at one time baking for the Austro-Hungarian Court. The *Emperor Torte*, which is to be found in this book, was her own creation and the favorite of Emperor Franz Josef. The majority, however, have been passed down in my family from mother to daughter and are thus my own valued heritage.

Many a housewife will perceive that these desserts require more eggs and more butter than she is generally accustomed to use—to say nothing of almonds and walnuts. It is precisely the ingredients required to prepare these desserts which bespeak their delicacy.

However, this increase in cost is hardly actual, for it will be discovered in the end that because of their richness, smaller portions must be served. The yield is therefore greater than is apparent at first.

Every recipe is of the kind which can be prepared by a homemaker in her kitchen with only little more effort than that required by an ordinary cake. All these recipes fall outside the category of desserts that require professional skill in their preparation.

Recipes for cookies, muffins, slices and sticks for the afternoon tea party have been included.

I recommend these desserts to other American hostesses with the sure knowledge that if she serves them, she will receive the same pleasant compliments I have when I have delighted my guests with these European specialties.

Preface

My gratitude is due Ruth P. Casa-Emellos, Home Economist of the New York *Times*, for the infinite pains she has taken in the editing of my manuscript.

ALICE SIDON

San Francisco, California May, 1950

IMPORTANT SUGGESTIONS

MIXING. Many recipes require very long beating of eggs or creamed mixtures. A cook of the old European school might not have winced at the thought of mixing by hand for an hour or so, but no modern woman in her right mind would subject herself to such an ordeal. Fortunately, the electric mixer can take over the job with equally fine results. It should be set at slow or medium speed. Mixtures are beaten till very thick and fluffy, rather than for a specified time. However, when the directions say to fold in sugar or flour, the mixer *must not be used*.

PANS OR FORMS. Cake pans or forms of the spring-form type with removable sides and bottom are almost necessary for successful handling of some of the products after baking. These pans in various sizes and depths are available in many housewares stores. When using one, always allow room for expansion of the batter. A spongecake type of batter doubles in volume and most tortes expand about one-third. Many recipes may be divided in half and smaller pans used. To grease pans, use the fat which rises to the top of butter that is melted (the sediment of melted butter will cause sticking), or use a solid shortening.

CHAPTER ONE

CAKES AND SLICES

APRICOT CAKE

⅔ cup sweet butter
¾ cup sugar
1 cup blanched almonds, ground
8 egg whites
8 egg yolks

1 teaspoon vanilla
1 scant cup cracker meal
1 pound fresh or stewed apricots
Confectioners' sugar

Cream butter and sugar. Mix almonds with two egg whites and add to creamed mixture. Blend well, add egg yolks gradually, then add vanilla and beat twenty minutes by hand or in electric beater till thick. Beat remaining six egg whites and fold lightly into almond mixture, adding cracker meal slowly at the same time. Pour into a buttered and floured 9 x 13-inch shallow pan and cover with halved apricots, skins down. Bake in a slow oven (300 degrees F.) for an hour. Before serving (preferably the following day) sprinkle with confectioners' sugar and cut into slices. Yield: approximately twenty-four slices.

FRENCH APRICOT OR PLUM CAKE

4¼ cups sifted flour
½ teaspoon salt
1 teaspoon baking powder
1⅓ cups sweet butter
¾ cup sugar
5 egg yolks

½ teaspoon grated
   lemon rind
¼ cup cream
2 to three pounds fresh
   apricots or plums,
   stoned

Combine flour, salt and baking powder and sift onto a kneading board. Cut in butter and make a depression in the center. Place in the depression sugar, egg yolks, lemon rind and cream. Mix with a knife or spoon to form a dough, then knead until it begins to blister. Place dough in a floured bowl, cover with a cloth and refrigerate for one hour. Place on a floured board and roll to fit a pan 10 x 17 inches which has been sprinkled with flour.

Halve fruit and arrange skinside-down on dough, leaving bare a one-inch rim on all four edges. Fold this rim in one-half inch toward the filling. Bake in a moderate oven (350 degrees F.) about forty-five minutes. When done sprinkle additional sugar over fruit and cut as desired. Yield: twenty servings.

FRENCH CHERRY CAKE

Prepare dough as for French Apricot or Plum Cake. Substitute two pounds of fresh cherries, pitted, for the apricots, covering the cake with them except for the one-inch margin. Bake as French Apricot or Plum Cake and sprinkle sugar generously over the cherries when done. Serve either warm or cold. Yield: about twenty servings.

FRENCH COTTAGE CHEESE CAKE

1 recipe dough for
French Apricot or
   Plum Cake (Page
   18)
5 tablespoons butter

$2/3$ cup sugar
1 pint dry cottage cheese
$1/3$ cup seedless raisins
1 egg
$1/4$ cup cream

Roll dough and place in a 10 x 17-inch floured pan. Cream butter and add one by one rest of ingredients in the order listed. Spread mixture on top of cake dough and bake as French Apricot or Plum Cake remembering to fold edges in one-half inch toward the cottage cheese spread. Yield: twenty servings.

FRENCH BUTTER CAKE

Prepare dough as for French Apricot or Plum Cake and arrange in pan. Brush with one beaten egg and sprinkle with a mixture of one-third cup finely chopped walnuts and two tablespoons sugar. Bake in a moderate oven (350 degrees F.) about thirty-five minutes. Cool before slicing. Yield: about twenty servings.

FRENCH COFFEE CAKE

¾ cup sweet butter

1 cup sugar

1 egg

1 teaspoon vanilla

2 cups sifted flour

1 teaspoon baking powder

½ cup jam or preserves

Cream butter thoroughly, add gradually sugar, egg and vanilla and mix for about fifteen minutes by hand or in electric mixer till thick. Combine flour and baking powder, sift and blend into mixture. Turn into a greased 8 x 13-inch pan and bake in a moderate oven (350 de-degrees F.) twenty-five to thirty minutes or until light brown. Cool cake, cover with jam or preserves and cut into two-inch squares. Yield: about two dozen squares.

FRUIT CAKE

½ cup sweet butter
1 cup sugar
3 eggs, separated
¾ cup sour milk or buttermilk
2 cups sifted flour

1 teaspoon baking soda
Rind of one lemon, grated
⅔ cup seedless raisins
⅔ cup dried figs, diced
⅔ cup dates, sliced
⅔ cup chopped walnuts

Cream butter with sugar, add egg yolks gradually while mixing. Add one-half the milk and then add flour. Dissolve baking soda in the rest of the milk and stir into mixture. Add gradually, grated lemon rind, raisins, figs, dates and chopped walnuts. Beat egg whites stiffly and fold into batter. Bake in a well-buttered loaf form in a moderate oven (350 degrees F.) about one hour. Yield: one loaf.

GERMAN COFFEE CAKE

½ cup sweet butter
½ cup sugar
4 eggs, separated
¼ cup milk

2 cups sifted flour
2 teaspoons baking powder
Rind of one lemon, grated
Powdered sugar

Cream butter with sugar, add gradually egg yolks and milk. Sift flour with baking powder and blend in

[**21**]

gradually. Add lemon rind and fold in stiffly beaten egg whites. Pour mixture into a deep buttered cake form and bake in a moderate oven (350 degrees F.) about forty-five minutes. Sprinkle with powdered sugar. Yield: ten to twelve servings.

HONEY CAKE I

3 eggs, separated
$\frac{2}{3}$ cup sugar
1 cup strained honey
$\frac{1}{2}$ cup chopped
  orange peel

$2\frac{3}{4}$ cups sifted flour
2 teaspoons baking powder
$\frac{1}{2}$ teaspoon cinnamon
$\frac{1}{2}$ teaspoon ground cloves
$\frac{1}{3}$ cup halved walnuts

Beat egg whites stiffly, add sugar gradually and continuing beating till mixture forms peaks. Add egg yolks one by one, blend in honey and orange peel, mixing thoroughly. Sift together flour, baking powder, cinnamon and cloves and blend into mixture. Pour batter into a well-buttered 5 x 9-inch loaf form, arrange the halved nuts on top of cake and bake in a slow oven (300 degrees F.) about one hour. Yield: one loaf.

Cakes and Slices

HONEY CAKE II

1 teaspoon baking soda
1/3 cup milk
4 1/2 cups sifted flour
2 eggs
1 cup strained honey
1 1/2 cup sugar
1 teaspoon cinnamon
1/3 cup chopped orange peel
1/2 cup chopped walnuts

Dissolve baking soda in milk and add to flour. Mix in gradually eggs, honey, sugar, cinnamon, orange peel and chopped walnuts. If batter seems too thick, add a little more milk. It should be a thick drop batter. Pour into a well-buttered 5 x 9-inch loaf form and bake in a slow oven (300 degrees F.) about one hour. Yield: one loaf.

LEMON CAKE

2/3 cup sweet butter
1 1/2 cups sugar
1/2 lemon
8 egg whites
1 1/4 cups flour
1 teaspoon baking powder
1/2 teaspoon almond extract

Cream butter and sugar thoroughly for about twenty minutes by hand or use an electric mixer. Add the grated

[**23**]

rind and juice of lemon. Beat egg whites stiffly and fold in. Sift together flour and baking powder, blend in and add almond extract. Pour into a buttered loaf form and bake about one hour in a slow oven (300 degrees F.). Cool, take out of form and store a day or longer before cutting. Yield: one loaf.

NUT ROLL

1 recipe Nut Filling (below)
5 eggs, separated
¼ cup sugar
½ cup walnuts, ground
½ pint heavy cream, whipped

Prepare filling and set aside. Cream egg yolks with sugar, then fold in stiffly beaten egg whites. Add walnuts to mixture. Pour into a buttered 8 x 13-inch shallow pan and bake twenty to twenty-five minutes or until light brown in a moderate oven (350 degrees F.). Turn out onto a damp cloth, spread filling over cake and roll as jelly roll while still hot. It is advisable to bake this roll the day before using. Cover with whipped cream before serving. Yield: eight to ten servings.

Nut Filling

~~~~~~

1 cup boiling milk   2⁄3 cup sugar
1½ cups walnuts, ground   1 tablespoon rum
2⁄3 cup sweet butter

Pour boiling milk over walnuts and cool. Cream butter with sugar, add walnut mixture and rum and mix thoroughly.

RAISIN CAKE

~~~~~~

2⁄3 cup sweet butter   6 egg whites
3⁄4 cup sugar   3⁄4 cup cracker meal
½ cup blanched almonds,   ½ cup seedless
  ground   raisins
8 egg yolks

Cream butter, add sugar, almonds and gradually the egg yolks. Mix for thirty minutes by hand or in an electric mixer till thick. Fold in stiffly beaten egg whites and fold in the cracker meal. Pour batter into a buttered and floured spring form. Sprinkle raisins on top. (The raisins will sink in the batter.) Bake in a slow oven (325 degrees F.) about one hour. Serve the following day. Yield: about twelve servings.

RUMANIAN SOUR CREAM CAKE

3 eggs

1¼ cups sugar

1 teaspoon vanilla

½ pint sour cream

1¾ cups sifted flour

1 teaspoon baking powder

1 teaspoon baking soda

2 tablespoons ground sweet chocolate

2 tablespoons ground walnuts

Cream eggs and sugar, add vanilla and sour cream and mix well. Sift together flour, baking powder and baking soda, add to batter and blend in. Pour half the batter into a 3½ x 9-inch greased loaf form, sprinkle with chocolate and walnuts and pour the remaining batter on top. Bake in a moderate oven (350 degrees F.) one hour. Yield: one loaf.

ALEXANDER SLICES

¾ cup sugar

8 egg yolks

1 cup blanched almonds, ground

5 egg whites

½ cup sifted flour

½ cup jam

Mix sugar and egg yolks thirty minutes by hand or beat till thick in electric mixer. Mix almonds with one egg white and add to mixture. Beat remaining egg whites stiffly and fold in. Blend flour in lightly. Pour into a buttered shallow pan and bake in a moderate oven (350 degrees F.) about twenty-five minutes. After it has cooled a little cover one half with jam, cut the other half and place on top of jam, then cover top with any icing desired and cut into slices. Yield: approximately three dozen slices.

ALMOND SLICES

¾ cup sugar
2 egg whites
1 cup blanched almonds, ground

¼ cup finely cut citron
Rice paper

Mix sugar, egg whites and almonds for one hour by hand or beat till thick in an electric mixer. Add citron. Place rice paper on a cookie sheet, spread with almond mixture and cut into one by one-and-one-half-inch strips about one-half inch thick. Place in a warm oven and let stay until slices have dried. (To prepare oven, heat to 300 degrees F. for about ten minutes then shut off the heat.) When cooled, cover slices with any desired icing. Yield: about two dozen slices.

HAZEL NUT SLICES

2 cups hazel nuts

½ cup sweet butter

1 cup sugar

4 egg whites

¼ cup flour

½ teaspoon baking powder

4 ounces sweet chocolate

Toast hazel nuts in a moderate oven (350 degrees F.) until skins peel off. Remove skins and grind the nuts. Cream butter and sugar thoroughly. Add unbeaten egg whites, then gradually mix in ground hazel nuts. Sift together flour and baking powder and blend in. Pour mixture into a well-buttered shallow 8 x 13-inch pan and bake in a moderate oven (350 degrees F.) about twenty-five minutes.

Melt chocolate in a double boiler and spread on cake. Cool cake completely and cut into slices. Yield: twenty-five to thirty slices.

FLORENTINE TORTELLETTES

¾ cup sugar

8 egg yolks

2 eggs

1¼ cups sifted flour

Mix sugar, egg yolks and eggs for thirty minutes by hand or beat till thick in electric mixer. Blend in flour quickly and bake in a well-buttered shallow pan for about fifteen minutes in a moderate oven (350 degrees

F.). Cool, cut into one by two and one-half-inch strips and cover evenly with Crème. Yield: about two dozen bars.

Crème Topping

4 egg yolks

1 egg

⅓ cup sugar

1 teaspoon vanilla

7 tablespoons sweet butter

Place egg yolks, egg, sugar and vanilla in a double boiler and, using an egg beater, beat continuously, cooking till mixture thickens. Mix in cooled melted butter and continue beating until completely cooled.

LOLA'S SLICES

2¼ cups sifted flour

1 teaspoon baking powder

2 cups blanched almonds, ground

1½ cups sugar

1 egg

2 egg yolks

Sift together flour and baking powder. Add almonds and sugar. Mix in egg and egg yolks and knead until dough is smooth. Roll to one-eighth inch thickness and cut into desired slices. Place on a cookie sheet and bake in a moderate oven (350 degrees F.) about fifteen minutes or until golden brown. Yield: four dozen slices.

ORANGE SLICES

1½ cups sugar

2 eggs

3 egg yolks

½ cup candied orange
and lemon peel

Rind of one-half lemon,
grated

2¼ cups sifted flour

1 teaspoon baking
powder

1 tablespoon powdered
sugar

Mix sugar, eggs and egg yolks for about fifteen minutes by hand or beat in electric mixer till thick. Add fruit peels, and lemon rind. Sift flour and baking powder together and blend into creamed mixture to form a firm dough. Roll to one-fourth inch thickness, cut into slices and place on a buttered cookie sheet. Bake in a moderate oven (350 degrees F.) fifteen to twenty minutes. Sprinkle with powdered sugar. Yield: about four dozen slices.

NUT SLICES

⅓ cup sweet butter
½ cup sugar
1¾ cups walnuts, ground

2 eggs
6 eggs, separated
1 cup plus two tablespoons zwieback crumbs

Cream butter with sugar, add walnuts, eggs and egg yolks gradually and mix for fifteen minutes by hand or in electric mixer till thick. Beat egg whites stiffly, fold into batter and blend in the crushed zwieback lightly. Pour into a buttered and floured shallow pan and bake in a slow oven (325 degrees F.) about twenty-five minutes. When cooled cover with lemon or any other icing and cut into squares or slices. Yield: about two dozen slices.

SACHER SLICES

¾ cup sweet butter

¾ cup sugar

5½ ounces sweet chocolate, melted

6 eggs, separated

1 teaspoon almond extract, optional

1¼ cups sifted flour

1 teaspoon baking powder

½ cup warm jam or preserves

2 tablespoons confectioners' sugar

Cream butter and sugar. Add chocolate and blend in the egg yolks, one by one. Beat the egg whites stiffly and fold in. Add almond extract. Combine flour and baking powder and blend in. Pour into a shallow buttered pan and bake in a moderate oven (350 degrees F.) about thirty-five to forty minutes.

While still hot, spread one half the cake with jam, cut off the uncovered half of the cake and lay it carefully on top of jam. When cooled, sprinkle with powdered sugar and cut into slices. Yield: twenty to twenty-five slices.

Cakes and Slices

TEA SLICES

¾ cup less one table-
    spoon sweet butter
¾ cup sugar
4 egg yolks
1 egg
1 teaspoon rum

1¼ cups sifted flour
1 egg white
⅓ cup sliced lemon peel
⅓ cup thinly shredded
    almonds
2 tablespoons sugar

Cream butter, add sugar, egg yolks and egg and mix for thirty minutes by hand or in electric mixer till thick. Add rum and flour and blend well. Spread mixture about one-eighth inch thick in a buttered 8 x 13-inch shallow pan. Beat egg white stiffly and spread over top. Mix lemon peel, almonds and sugar and sprinkle over egg whites. Bake in a slow oven (300 degrees F.) about fifteen minutes. Cut into slices while still warm. Yield: about thirty slices.

CHAPTER TWO

COOKIES

ALMOND COOKIES

~~~~~~~~~~~~~~~~~~~~~~~~~~~~~~~~~~~~~~

1 cup sweet butter
2⅓ cups sifted flour
2⅓ cups almonds, ground
1⅔ cups sugar

⅓ cup ground sweet chocolate
3 eggs
½ cup finely chopped almonds

Cut butter into small pieces and rub into flour on a kneading board. Add almonds and then add, gradually, sugar, chocolate, whole egg and two egg yolks. Knead until dough is smooth. Place in a floured bowl, cover and let stand in refrigerator thirty minutes. Roll dough about one-eighth inch thick on a floured board.

Cut into small squares or any desired cookie shape, brush with remaining egg whites and sprinkle with chopped almonds. Place on greased cookie sheets and bake about fifteen minutes in a moderate oven (350 degrees F.). Remove cookies carefully with a knife or spatula. Yield: four to five dozen cookies.

Cookies

COOKIES À LA BUDAPEST

8 egg whites
1¼ cups sugar
2 cups almonds, ground

½ teaspoon cinnamon
1 tablespoon ground
    chocolate

Beat egg whites stiffly, add sugar and cook over water while using an egg beater continuously until mixture is heated. Add almonds and continue beating until mixture is thoroughly heated and thickened. Remove from heat. Mix cinnamon and chocolate and add. Drop by small spoonfuls into pans lined with buttered waxed paper. Bake in a very slow oven (250 degrees F.) fifteen to twenty minutes. Yield: about two and one-half dozen cookies.

BUTTER RINGS

1¼ cups sweet butter
2½ cups sifted flour
2 eggs, separated
½ cup sugar
½ teaspoon vanilla

Grated rind of one-half
    lemon
½ cup chopped walnuts
2 tablespoons sugar

Cut butter into flour, add egg yolks, sugar, vanilla and grated lemon rind. Knead until dough is smooth.

[35]

Roll half the dough at a time (chill balance till ready to roll) on a floured board to one-eighth inch thickness. Cut in ring forms, brush with egg whites and sprinkle with walnuts which have been mixed with sugar. Bake on buttered cookie sheets fifteen to twenty minutes in a moderate oven (350 degrees F.) until light brown. Remove from pan after rings have cooled slightly. Yield: about four dozen cookies.

CHEESE COOKIES

1 cup milk	4½ ounces grated
6 tablespoons sweet butter	Parmesan cheese
1 cup sifted flour	Pinch of salt
4 eggs	

Bring milk and butter to a boil. Add flour, stirring constantly, and continue cooking and stirring until batter no longer sticks to pan. Pour into a mixing bowl and stir until cooled. Mix in gradually three eggs, Parmesan cheese (reserving two tablespoons) and salt. Drop by heaping teaspoonfuls on buttered cookie sheets. Beat remaining egg and use to brush over cookies. Bake in a moderate oven (350 degrees F.) about thirty minutes or until light brown. Remove from sheet when slightly cooled and sprinkle reserved Parmesan cheese on top.

Cookies

These cookies taste better when served warm and are delicious as hors d'oeuvre. Yield: two dozen cookies.

CHERRY COOKIES

1¼ cups sweet butter
2¼ cups sifted flour
⅔ cup sugar
1 tablespoon lemon juice
1 cup blanched almonds, ground

10 hard-cooked egg yolks, sieved
1 egg
4 dozen glazed cherries

Rub small pieces of butter with flour between hands until well mixed. Add sugar and lemon juice. Add almonds and egg yolks and knead until dough is smooth. Cover and let stand in refrigerator one hour. Using half the batch at a time, roll on a floured board to about one-fourth inch thickness. Cut into rounds about one and one-half inches in diameter and make a dent with forefinger in center of each cookie. Lift carefully with a spatula, place on buttered cookie sheets, brush with beaten egg and bake in a moderate oven (350 degrees F.) about fifteen minutes or until light brown. Remove carefully, cool and place a glazed cherry in the center of each cookie. Yield: four dozen cookies.

CHOCOLATE CONES

1 cup sugar	1 egg white
1 tablespoon ground chocolate	Rice paper
	$\frac{1}{3}$ cup diced almonds
2 tablespoons lemon juice	2 tablespoons sugar

Mix well sugar, chocolate and lemon juice. Beat white of egg stiffly and fold in. Cover bottom of pan with wafer or rice paper. Shape teaspoons of the mixture into cones on the wafer paper. Mix diced almonds with sugar and sprinkle on cones. Place in a barely warm oven till completely dry, about two hours. When done trim paper from around bottoms. Yield: one dozen cones.

CINNAMON STICKS

8 egg whites	2 cups blanched almonds
$1\frac{1}{2}$ cups sugar	$\frac{1}{4}$ cup cinnamon
$\frac{1}{2}$ lemon	

Beat whites of eggs stiffly, blend in sugar and add grated lemon rind and juice. Chop almonds finely, mix with cinnamon and add. Form sticks about three inches long, one-half inch wide and about one-half inch thick and arrange on buttered cookie sheets. Bake in a moderate oven (350 degrees F.) about fifteen minutes or until golden brown. Yield: two dozen cookies.

ENGLISH TEA COOKIES

3¾ cups sifted flour
½ teaspoon baking soda
4 tablespoons sweet
   butter

2 tablespoons sour
   cream
3 eggs
1¼ cups sugar

Sift together flour and baking soda and cut butter into mixture. Add gradually sour cream, eggs and sugar. Add enough more cream to make a stiff dough. Knead until dough is smooth. Roll on a floured board to one-eighth inch thickness and cut into any desired cookie shapes. Bake on buttered cookie sheets in a moderate oven (350 degrees F.) about fifteen minutes, or until light brown. This recipe will turn out a large batch of cookies which can be kept almost indefinitely.

FRENCH FILBERT STICKS

1¾ cups filberts, ground
1¼ cups sugar
3 egg whites

2 tablespoons powdered sugar
1 teaspoon vanilla

Mix filberts with sugar and two egg whites. Knead dough on a floured board and roll to one-eighth inch thickness. Cut sticks about two inches long and three-fourths inch wide and place carefully on buttered cookie sheets. Beat remaining egg whites stiffly, blend in powdered sugar and vanilla to make a meringue. Pour a thin layer of meringue from a teaspoon on each stick. Bake in a slow oven (300 degrees F.) about ten minutes. Yield: four dozen sticks.

FRENCH TEA COOKIES

⅔ cup salted butter
2 cups sifted flour
4 egg yolks

1 tablespoon cream
Pinch of salt
2 egg whites

Cut butter into flour. Add egg yolks, cream and salt and knead until dough is smooth. Chill in refrigerator for one hour. Roll lightly on a floured board, fold over once, then fold again crosswise and return to refrigerator for another hour. Roll dough to finger thickness, cut into rounds and place on buttered cookie sheets. Brush tops with egg whites, bake in a moderate oven (350 degrees F.) about thirty minutes, or until light brown. Remove carefully when cooled. Yield: four dozen cookies.

HONEY KISSES

2½ cups sifted flour
1 cup sugar
2 eggs
2 tablespoons strained honey

1 teaspoon baking soda
¼ cup milk
½ teaspoon cinnamon
½ cup blanched almonds

Mix flour thoroughly with sugar and eggs, then add honey. Dissolve baking soda in milk and add to mixture. Stir in cinnamon. Cover bowl and let dough rest for two hours. Take level tablespoons of dough and make kisses by rolling each between palms. Arrange on buttered cookie sheets and make slight dents on tops with finger. Place an almond in each dent. Bake in a moderate oven (350 degrees F.) about twenty minutes. Yield: about five dozen kisses.

HUNGARIAN COOKIES

~~~~~~~~~~~~~~~~~~~~~~~~~~~~~~~~~~~~~

6 tablespoons sweet butter

½ cup sugar

1 egg

2 eggs, separated

1 cup sifted flour

1 teaspoon cinnamon

½ cup chopped walnuts

Cream butter, add gradually sugar, egg and egg yolks. Sift together flour and cinnamon. Add to creamed mixture and knead until dough is smooth. Place in a bowl, cover and let stand in refrigerator for one-half hour. Roll to one-eighth inch thickness on a floured board. Cut into cookie shapes, brush with egg whites and sprinkle with chopped walnuts. Arrange on buttered cookie sheets and bake in a moderate oven (350 degrees F.) about fifteen minutes. Remove cookies with a knife or spatula. Yield: about two and one-half dozen cookies.

HUSSAR BALLS

~~~~~~~~~~~~~~~~~~~~~~~~~~~~~~~~~~~~~

⅔ cup sweet butter

⅓ cup sugar

1 egg yolk

2 eggs

1¼ cups sifted flour

⅓ cup diced almonds

⅓ cup jam

Cream butter with sugar, add egg yolk and one egg and mix well. Blend in flour. Break off walnut-sized pieces of dough and form balls between palms. Place on a buttered cookie sheet and use forefinger to make a deep well on top of each ball. Brush balls with remaining egg, beaten, sprinkle almonds around the well and bake in a moderate oven (350 degrees F.) about twenty minutes. Cool balls and fill wells with jam. Yield: about three dozen balls.

ISCHLER TORTELLETTES

2 cups sifted flour	¾ cup sugar
1 teaspoon baking powder	Juice of one-half lemon
	½ cup jam
1 cup sweet butter	4 ounces sweet chocolate
1 cup almonds, ground	

Sift flour with baking powder on a kneading board. Cut small pieces of butter into flour, add almonds, sugar and lemon juice and knead till dough is smooth. Chill half the dough. Roll remaining dough to about one-eighth inch thickness and cut into round cookie shapes. Place cookies on floured cookie sheets and bake ten to fifteen minutes or until light brown in a moderately hot oven (375 degrees F.). Repeat with second half of dough.

Remove cookies carefully and, after cooling, spread jam between two cookies until all cookies are paired. Melt chocolate over hot water and cover tortellettes with a thin coating. Yield: two dozen cookies.

JAM COOKIES

⅔ cup sweet butter	1 teaspoon vanilla
1½ cups sifted flour	⅓ cup jam
⅓ cup sugar	2 tablespoons powdered
2 egg yolks	sugar

Cut butter into flour and knead in sugar, egg yolks and vanilla. When dough is smooth roll to one-eighth inch thickness on a floured board. Cut into small rounds and bake on buttered cookie sheets fifteen to twenty minutes in a moderate oven (350 degrees F.) until a very light brown. Cool cookies before removing from pans. Spread jam on bottom part of one cookie and cover with bottom part of another cookie. Continue until all cookies are paired, then sprinkle with powdered sugar. Yield: two dozen cookies.

Cookies

LEMON KISSES

~~~~~~

1 egg white   Grated rind of one-half lemon
¾ cup sugar   ¾ cup ground almonds or walnuts

Mix egg white with sugar and beat until stiff. Add rest of ingredients and mix well. Line a cookie pan with waxed paper and drop level tablespoons of mixture to form kisses. Bake in a slow oven (300 degrees F.) about fifteen minutes or until very light brown. Cool and remove from pan. Yield: about eighteen kisses.

LONDON STICKS

~~~~~~

⅔ cup sweet butter   2 egg yolks
1½ cups sifted flour   ½ cup jam
⅓ cup sugar

Cut butter into flour, add sugar and egg yolks. Knead dough on a floured board and roll to one-eighth inch thickness. Place dough on a buttered cookie sheet, spread jam on top and cover with Chocolate Almond Topping. Bake in a moderate oven (350 degrees F.) about twenty minutes. Cool slightly and cut into sticks. Yield: about two and one-half dozen sticks.

Chocolate Almond Topping

3 egg whites   4 ounces sweet chocolate,
1 cup sugar   melted
⅓ cup almonds

Beat egg whites stiffly, mix in sugar and ground almonds. Fold in chocolate.

MACAROONS

1 cup blanched almonds,   1¼ cups sugar
     ground   ½ teaspoon vanilla
2 egg whites

Mix almonds with one egg white. Add sugar, vanilla and remaining egg white and mix about forty-five minutes or beat in electric mixer till stiff. Drop by teaspoonfuls on cookie pans which have been lined with buttered waxed paper. Bake about fifteen minutes in a slow oven (300 degrees F.). Yield: one and one-half dozen macaroons.

Cookies

DARK MACAROONS

¾ cup almonds, ground	⅔ cup sugar
	⅓ cup ground chocolate
1 egg white	½ lemon

Grind almonds and mix with egg white. Add sugar, chocolate, lemon juice and the grated rind. Mix thoroughly until ingredients are blended. Drop by teaspoonfuls on a baking sheet which has been covered with buttered waxed paper. Bake about fifteen minutes in a moderate oven (350 degrees F.). Yield: one and one-half dozen macaroons.

MERINGUE KISSES

2½ cups sugar	1 tablespoon lemon juice
7 egg whites	1 cup halved walnuts

Mix sugar, egg whites and lemon juice in a double boiler and cook, beating with an egg beater, until mixture becomes thick and stiff. Place buttered waxed paper on a cookie sheet and arrange halved walnuts about two inches apart on the paper. Cover each walnut with one tablespoonful of mixture. Bake in a slow oven (300 degrees F.) ten to fifteen minutes or until kisses begin to brown. Cool and remove with a knife or spatula. Yield: four dozen kisses.

NON PLUS ULTRA COOKIES

1¼ cups butter   2 egg whites
2 cups sifted flour   ¾ cup sugar
2 tablespoons sugar   ½ cup jam
3 egg yolks

Cut small pieces of butter into sifted flour. Add two tablespoons sugar and egg yolks and knead till smooth. Roll to one-eighth inch thickness on a floured board and cut into round cookies. Place on buttered cookie sheets and cover with meringue made by beating egg whites with three-fourths cup sugar. Bake in a slow oven (300 degrees F.) fifteen to twenty minutes. Cool cookies and spread jam between bottoms of each two until all cookies are paired. Yield: three and one-half dozen cookies.

NUT CONES

1½ cups walnuts, ground   1 cup sugar
¾ cup hazel nuts, ground   2 egg whites
1 teaspoon powdered coffee   Rice paper

Cookies

Mix walnuts, hazel nuts, coffee and three-fourths cup sugar. Beat egg whites stiffly and fold in. Cover bottom of pan with rice paper, shape teaspoons of mixture into cones on the paper. Sprinkle with remaining sugar and dry in a barely warm oven. When the surface is dry, the cones are done. Trim paper from bottoms. Yield: two and one-half dozen cones.

COOKIES À LA ROTHSCHILD

1 cup less two tablespoons
   sweet butter
$\frac{3}{4}$ cup sugar
4 egg yolks

1 cup sifted flour
$\frac{1}{2}$ cup jam
4 ounces sweet
   chocolate

Cream butter, add sugar gradually and add, one by one, the egg yolks. Add flour. Cover cookie sheets with buttered waxed paper. Take out one teaspoonful dough at a time and form a ball between the palms. Arrange on waxed paper, flatten with the hand and bake in a moderate oven (350 degrees F.) about fifteen minutes or until light brown. Cool, spread jam between each two cookies. Melt chocolate in a double boiler, cover tops of doubled cookies and let stand till dry. Yield: one and one-half dozen cookies.

PRUNE CROQUETTES

6 tablespoons sweet butter

4 egg yolks

1/4 pound dried prunes, cooked

1 cup blanched almonds, ground

1/2 cup sugar

2 slices white bread

Grated rind of one-half lemon

2 eggs

3/4 cup cracker meal

1/2 cup shortening

Cream butter and add egg yolks, one by one. Add the prunes which have been finely chopped. Mix in almonds and add sugar. Add bread which has been soaked in water and squeezed out. Add lemon rind. Form small balls or sausage shapes out of the mixture and place on a floured board. Dip croquettes in beaten eggs, roll in cracker meal and fry in hot shortening. Yield: six servings.

CHOCOLATE-COATED PRUNE CROQUETTES

Roll hot fried croquettes in a mixture of one-half cup ground sweet chocolate and one-fourth cup sugar.

Cookies

SUGAR PRETZELS

⅔ cup sweet butter	¾ cup sugar
1 cup sifted flour	1 egg
6 hard-cooked egg yolks, sieved	⅓ cup chopped walnuts
	2 tablespoons sugar

Cut butter into flour, add egg yolks and sugar. Knead into a smooth dough and chill in the refrigerator thirty minutes. Cut small pieces of dough about the size of a walnut and, on a floured board, roll with the hand to pencil thickness. Form pretzels and place on buttered cookie sheets. Beat the remaining egg and brush tops of pretzels. Mix walnuts with two tablespoons sugar and sprinkle over pretzels. Bake in a moderate oven (350 degrees F.) about fifteen minutes or until light brown. Cool before removing from pan. Yield: two and one-half dozen pretzels.

Continental Dessert Delicacies

TEA COOKIES

1 cup less two tablespoons sweet butter
2¼ cups sifted flour

½ cup sugar
1 egg
½ cup jam

Cut butter into flour, add sugar and egg and knead to a smooth dough. Roll to one-eighth inch thickness on a floured board. Place dough on a buttered cookie sheet and bake in a moderate oven (350 degrees F.) about twenty minutes, until light brown. Cut, while still hot, into small squares. Cool cookies, take out of pan and spread jam between each two cookies. Yield: about three dozen cookies.

TEA STICKS

6 tablespoons sweet butter
1½ cups sugar
1¾ cups sifted flour

1 cup boiling water
12 egg yolks

Cream butter and one and one-fourth cups sugar in a saucepan. Blend in flour, place over low heat and, while stirring, pour boiling water over mixture. Continue cooking and stirring until mixture thickens and batter no longer sticks to pan. Remove from heat, cool completely, and add egg yolks one by one. Place dough on a floured board and, if too sticky, use a little flour. Cut off small pieces of dough and form sticks, rounds, or pretzels. Place on a buttered cookie sheet, brush with water and sprinkle with remaining one-fourth cup sugar. Bake in a moderate oven (350 degrees F.) about fifteen minutes or until light brown. Yield: two and one-half dozen cookies.

TEA ZWIEBACK

1 cup sifted flour
¾ cup sugar
2 eggs

1 egg yolk
¼ cup chopped almonds

Form a smooth dough on a kneading board by blending flour, sugar, one egg and the egg yolk. Fit dough into a buttered 3½ x 9-inch loaf pan and brush top with remaining egg, well beaten. Sprinkle with almonds and bake in a moderate oven (350 degrees F.) about forty minutes. Slice while still warm. Arrange slices on a cookie sheet and dry in a slow oven (250 degrees F.) about ten minutes or until slices are lightly browned. Yield: about eighteen slices.

TORTELLETTES

⅔ cup sweet butter   ¾ cup sugar
1⅓ cups sifted flour   1 egg
1 cup almonds, ground

Cut butter into flour. Add almonds, sugar and egg. Knead until dough is smooth and chill in refrigerator for fifteen minutes. Roll dough on a floured board to about one-eighth inch thickness, cut into rounds and place on buttered cookie sheets. Bake fifteen minutes in a moderate oven (350 degrees F.). Cool slightly, remove, place tortellettes on a board and cover with lemon icing. Yield: five dozen cookies.

Lemon Icing

1¼ cups confec-   1 teaspoon sweet butter, or
    tioners' sugar   1 tablespoon cream
3 tablespoons lemon
    juice

Sift sugar into a bowl, add strained lemon juice and blend until smooth. Add butter and mix well. If icing is too thick add a little table cream; if too thin add a little more confectioners' sugar.

Cookies

VANILLA CRESCENTS

⅔ cup sweet butter   ¼ cup sugar
1⅔ cup sifted flour   1 teaspoon vanilla
½ cup almonds,   1 cup confectioners' sugar
  ground

Cut butter into flour, add almonds and knead. Add sugar and vanilla and knead until dough is smooth. Take a teaspoonful of dough out at a time, roll between palms and form crescents. Bake on a buttered cookie sheet in a moderate oven (350 degrees F.) about fifteen minutes or until light brown. Place confectioners' sugar on a sheet of paper on a board and roll slightly cooled crescents in the sugar till they are completely covered. It should be noted that if crescents are rolled in sugar while too hot they will break, and if they are cold the sugar will not adhere. Yield: about three dozen crescents.

WALNUT CRESCENTS

3¾ cups sifted flour	2 eggs
1 tablespoon baking powder	1 cup sugar
	¼ cup milk
⅔ cup butter	1 teaspoon white vinegar

Sift flour with baking powder and cut in butter. Add gradually eggs, sugar, milk and vinegar and knead until dough is smooth. Roll to one-eighth inch thickness, cut into two-inch squares and place about a half teaspoonful of walnut filling in middle of each square.

Fold a corner of a square in about half way so that folded corner will cover filling, then roll the triangle and bend it in the shape of a crescent. Place on a buttered cookie sheet and bake in a moderate oven (350 degrees F.) about twenty minutes or until light brown. Yield: about four dozen crescents.

Walnut Filling

1 cup broken walnuts	6 tablespoons sugar
⅓ cup hot milk	2 teaspoons rum

Grind walnuts, pour boiling milk over them and mix in rest of ingredients.

CHAPTER THREE

CRÈMES AND GELATIN DESSERTS

CRÈME À L'ANGLAISE

½ cup white wine
6 egg yolks
¾ cup sugar
1 tablespoon unflavored
  gelatin

¼ cup lukewarm water
½ pint cream, whipped

Cook wine, egg yolks and sugar in a double boiler, beating constantly until mixture becomes foamy and light. Add gelatin which has been softened in the water. Remove from heat and continue beating until cooled. Fold in the whipped cream, pour into a wetted form, or into individual molds and chill till firm. Yield: eight to ten servings.

APPLE À LA CRÈME

12 egg yolks
¾ cup sugar
2 tablespoons sifted
   flour
½ pint cream

1 cup almonds, ground
4 egg whites
8 to ten small apples
6 tablespoons jam

Mix in a double boiler eight egg yolks, sugar, flour and cream and cook, stirring, until thickened. Cool quickly, stirring occasionally. Add almonds. Mix in gradually remaining four egg yolks. Beat whites of eggs stiffly and fold in.

Peel and core apples, place in a buttered glass baking dish and fill cavities with jam. Pour custard mixture over apples and bake in a slow oven (300 degrees F.) one hour. Serve warm or cold, allowing one apple per serving.

CARAMEL CRÈME I

6 egg yolks
1 cup sugar
1 teaspoon cornstarch
1½ cups milk
Caramel

2 tablespoons unflavored
   gelatin
¼ cup lukewarm water
¾ cup heavy cream,
   whipped

Cook egg yolks, sugar, cornstarch and milk in a double boiler, whipping with a rotary beater until mixture thickens. Take from heat and add caramel, mixing it in immediately. Soften gelatin in lukewarm water, add and stir till dissolved. Cool crème and blend in whipped cream. Pour into a wetted pudding form or individual molds and chill in refrigerator till firm. Yield: eight to ten servings.

Caramel

1 cup sugar   ½ cup water

Cook sugar and water in a heavy saucepan, stirring, over low heat until light brown. Do not let it brown too much or caramel will be bitter. On the other hand, if not browned enough, caramel taste will be lacking.

CARAMEL CRÈME II

½ pint whipping   ¼ cup chopped walnuts
   cream   2 tablespoons unflavored
⅔ cup sugar   gelatin
Caramel (above)   ⅓ cup lukewarm water

Whip cream till stiff and mix in sugar. Add caramel in a fine stream while beating and add chopped walnuts.

Soften gelatin in lukewarm water, heat, stirring, till dissolved and blend into mixture. Pour into a wetted pudding form or individual molds and chill till firm. Yield: six to eight servings.

FRESH CHERRY CRÈME

1 pound fresh cherries
½ cup white wine
¼ cup sugar
2 egg yolks
1 tablespoon unflavored gelatin

⅓ cup lukewarm water
½ cup heavy cream, whipped

Pit cherries and cook in wine with sugar until soft and pulpy. Pass through a sieve and cool. Beat egg yolks, add to cooled mixture and cook in a double boiler, beating until thickened. Soften gelatin in the water and stir into hot mixture. Chill till syrupy and fold in cream. Pour into a wetted pudding form or individual molds and chill till set. Turn out and serve with additional whipped cream. Yield: six servings.

CHOCOLATE CRÈME

6 egg yolks	2 tablespoons unflavored
1½ cups milk	gelatin
1 cup sugar	½ cup lukewarm water
1 tablespoon corn-	⅓ cup ground chocolate
starch	¾ cup cream, whipped

Cook egg yolks, milk, sugar and cornstarch in a double boiler, beating with rotary beater until mixture thickens. Add gelatin which has been softened in the water. Stir in chocolate and let mixture cool. Chill till syrupy. Fold in whipped cream, turn into a wetted mold and chill till set. Yield: ten servings.

COFFEE CRÈME

Substitute one-third cup very strong black coffee for the ground chocolate.

CRÈME NOISETTE

Substitute one-half cup hazel nuts, toasted and chopped, for the ground chocolate.

FRUIT CRÈME

⅓ cup sifted flour
¾ cup sugar
1 cup milk
8 eggs, separated

½ pound fresh peaches
  or apricots
1 tablespoon sugar

Sift flour into a double boiler, add sugar and milk and mix until smooth. Cook, stirring, until mixture thickens. Remove from heat and continue stirring until cooled. Add egg yolks gradually, then fold in stiffly beaten egg whites. Halve peaches or apricots and arrange skinside-down in a buttered casserole. Sprinkle sugar on fruit and then pour crème mixture on top. Bake in a slow oven (300 degrees F.) about forty minutes. Serve warm. Yield: eight to ten servings.

ORANGE CRÈME

⅔ cup sugar
½ cup orange marmalade
1 cup orange juice
2 envelopes unflavored gelatin

½ cup lukewarm water
1 cup cream, whipped
1 to two cups fresh or canned tangerine sections

Mix sugar, marmalade and orange juice. Soften gelatin in the water, heat, stirring till dissolved and add to mixture. Cool till syrupy. Fold in whipped cream. Arrange tangerine segments in bottom of a wetted form, pour crème on top and chill till firm. Yield: eight to ten servings.

PINEAPPLE CRÈME

1 cup cream, whipped
⅔ cup sugar
½ cup pineapple juice
¼ cup crushed pine-
apple

1 tablespoon unflavored
gelatin
⅓ cup lukewarm water

Mix whipped cream, sugar, pineapple juice and crushed pineapple. Soften gelatin in lukewarm water, heat, stirring, till dissolved and stir into mixture. Pour into a wetted pudding form or individual molds and chill till firm. Yield: six to eight servings.

CRÈME AU RHUM

1¼ cups sugar
Juice of two oranges
Juice of two lemons
6 egg yolks
½ cup white wine

3 to four tablespoons rum
1½ tablespoons unflavored gelatin
¼ cup cool water
⅔ cup cream, whipped

Combine in a double boiler sugar, fruit juices, egg yolks, wine and rum. Place over heat and, using egg beater, beat continuously while cooking until foamy and thickened. Remove from heat and add gelatin which has been softened in the water. Cool till syrupy. Fold in whipped cream. Pour into a wetted form or individual glasses and chill in refrigerator. Yield: ten to twelve servings.

VANILLA CRÈME

6 egg yolks
1 cup sugar
1 teaspoon cornstarch
1½ cups milk
1 teaspoon vanilla

2 tablespoons unflavored gelatin
½ cup lukewarm water
¾ cup cream, whipped

Mix in a double boiler egg yolks, sugar, cornstarch, milk and vanilla. Cook, beating constantly, until mixture thickens. Take from heat and add gelatin which has been softened in lukewarm water. Cool till syrupy and blend in the whipped cream. Pour into a wetted pudding form or individual molds and chill till firm. Turn out of form before serving and, if desired, dress with whipped cream. Yield: six to eight servings.

JELLIED CHOCOLATE PUDDING

5 ounces sweet chocolate
5 tablespoons sugar
1/3 cup milk
1/2 teaspoon vanilla
1 tablespoon unflavored gelatin
4 tablespoons rum
1/2 pint whipping cream

Melt chocolate, add sugar, milk and vanilla and cook in a double boiler, stirring occasionally, until smooth. Soften gelatin in rum, add to chocolate mixture and stir till dissolved. Cool till syrupy and fold in whipped cream. Pour mixture into a wetted form or individual forms and refrigerate for at least six hours. If desired, add small pieces of candied fruit and dress with whipped cream. Yield: six servings.

JELLIED COFFEE PUDDING

$\frac{1}{3}$ cup sifted flour
2 cups milk
1 cup very strong hot
   coffee

$1\frac{1}{4}$ cups sugar
2 tablespoons unflavored
   gelatin
$\frac{1}{2}$ cup lukewarm water

Sift flour into a double boiler. Stir in milk gradually so as not to form lumps. Cook, stirring, until mixture thickens. Mix separately coffee, sugar and gelatin, which has been softened in lukewarm water. Combine with first mixture. Pour into a wetted form and chill in refrigerator. Serve with whipped cream or melted marshmallows. Yield: six to eight servings.

CHAPTER FOUR

PASTRIES

BACLAVA

4 cups sifted flour	1 cup lukewarm water,
1 teaspoon salt	approximately
1 cup sweet butter	2½ cups walnuts, ground
2 eggs	

Sift flour and salt onto a board and cut five table-spoons of butter into it. Make a depression in the middle and break eggs into it. Mix with a knife or spoon to make a dough, adding water a little at a time, and using enough to give a soft dough. Knead dough until it no longer sticks to the hands. Sprinkle board with flour and resume kneading until dough begins to blister—about thirty minutes. Cover with a warm napkin or a warm bowl and keep in a warm place for thirty minutes.

Spread a cloth on a table (about the size of a dining room table) and sprinkle generously with flour. Place half of the dough in the middle of the table and roll it to about the size of a dinner plate then start pulling dough carefully by the edges, in a circle, little by little, until dough is stretched to thinness of cigarette paper. To pull dough properly, keep thumbs inside palms, fingers of both hands close together and pointing toward each other with the dough resting on top of index fingers. Pull gently, in a circle, with a slight lifting motion. Trim off thick edges, using scissors. Let the stretched dough dry for a few minutes and in the meantime melt remaining butter. Cut dough into sheets or leaves that will fit a shallow 10 x 15-inch baking pan.

Brush pan with melted butter, place three or four layers of dough in bottom of pan, sprinkling or brushing each with melted butter. Cover with a thin layer of walnuts, then with one single layer of the stretched dough, apply melted butter, and cover again with a thin layer of walnuts. Continue to place alternately one dough-leaf, treated with melted butter, and one layer of walnuts until all the leaves are thus used.

Roll and stretch the second half of dough, let it dry a little, cut into layers as before and continue placing alternate layers of dough, melted butter and walnuts in the pan until all except three or four layers of dough have been used. Place the last three or four leaves, one on top of another, to form the top of baclava, brush each leaf with melted butter.

Dip a knife in hot butter and cut baclava lengthwise

and then across into strips that will form diamond or rectangular-shaped individual pieces about 3½ x 1½ inches. Pour a few tablespoons of melted butter into the knife slits, between the strips. Bake in a very slow oven (250 degrees F.) for about one hour. When baclava begins to turn light brown, pour boiling hot sugar syrup over it and let it bake a few minutes longer or until the syrup has penetrated. Take out baclavas, place on platter and pour a little more syrup on top. Baclavas are at their best if prepared one or two days before serving. Yield: about thirty baclavas.

Sugar Syrup

2½ cups sugar   2 teaspoons vanilla
2 cups water

Cook sugar, water and vanilla over low heat till syrupy, stirring till sugar is dissolved.

APPLE STRUDEL

2 cups sifted flour   ½ cup lukewarm water,
½ teaspoon salt   approximately
½ cup butter   2 tablespoons cracker meal
1 egg   Confectioners' sugar

Prepare dough as in Baclava (above), using two tablespoons of the butter. Stretch the entire batch without halving it. After dough has been stretched as thin as possible, melt the remainder of the butter and sprinkle it generously over the whole sheet of dough, using a brush. Sprinkle with cracker meal, and cover with apple filling.

Roll apple covered dough as jelly roll by lifting table cloth at one end and thus helping it to roll toward the opposite end. Cut the roll of strudel into lengths to fit into a well-buttered 8 x 13-inch shallow pan. Sprinkle strudel lightly with melted butter. Bake in a moderate oven (375 degrees F.) for twenty-five to thirty minutes or until light brown. When cooled cut into slices as desired and take out of pan. Sprinkle lightly with confectioners' sugar. Yield: fifteen to twenty slices.

CHERRY STRUDEL

Substitute three pounds of pitted fresh cherries for apples. Omit raisins and walnuts and scatter a mixture of sugar and cinnamon over the fruit.

Apple Filling

~~~~~~

6 large apples	½ cup seedless raisins
6 tablespoons sugar	1 tablespoon cinnamon
2 tablespoons ground walnuts	

Peel apples and whittle into thin shavings. Sprinkle over strudel dough. Mix sugar, walnuts, raisins and cinnamon and scatter over apples.

PEAR STRUDEL

~~~~~~

Substitute pears for apples in above recipe.

COTTAGE CHEESE STRUDEL

~~~~~~

Prepare dough as for Apple Strudel (above) and let stand under a warm bowl forty-five minutes instead of thirty. Fill with Cottage Cheese Filling and bake as Apple Strudel. If desired, serve with sour cream. Yield: about twenty servings.

¾ cup sugar

6 eggs, separated

½ teaspoon salt

1½ pints dry cottage cheese

½ cup seedless raisins

½ teaspoon cinnamon

½ teaspoon vanilla

Mix sugar and egg yolks. Add gradually and blend in salt, cottage cheese, raisins, cinnamon and vanilla. Beat egg whites stiffly and fold in lightly.

FEUILLETAGE I (FRENCH BUTTER DOUGH OR PUFF PASTE)

2 cups and two tablespoons sifted flour

¼ teaspoon salt

1¼ cups sweet butter

2 egg yolks

1 tablespoon lemon juice

½ cup cold water

Sift flour and salt together. Then place one-third on a kneading board. Cut butter into small pieces and let it fall into the flour. Roll with a rolling pin until all the flour has been absorbed by the butter. Lift this rolled paste onto a floured pan and place in the refrigerator.

Place rest of flour on a kneading board, make a depression in the middle and in it put the egg yolks and the lemon juice. Blend with a knife, adding water gradually. Knead dough with both hands till it begins to blister, sprinkling board and hands with small amounts of flour, if needed. (Use only enough flour to prevent sticking, not enough to harden dough.) Roll this dough into the same shape and size as that of the butter paste.

Place chilled butter mixture on top of dough on the board so that the narrow ends are to right and left. Fold over, doubling dough from right to left, then fold into thirds in the opposite direction so as to have three folds of the doubled paste. Roll the dough from the middle to the right and left, until it can be doubled and folded as previously, then place it on a floured pan and return to the refrigerator for fifteen minutes. Repeat this procedure—rolling, doubling and folding—three times, returning dough to refrigerator for fifteen minutes after each folding.

Use half the Feuilletage at a time, keeping the second half carefully wrapped in the refrigerator, for as long as two weeks. Feuilletage handles best when thoroughly chilled.

To insure puffing of Feuilletage in the following recipes do not brush the edges with beaten egg or with any other liquid unless so directed.

FEUILLETAGE II (FRENCH BUTTER DOUGH OR PUFF PASTE)

Feuilletage II is satisfactory for recipes requiring French Butter Dough but it does not puff as much as Feuilletage I.

2 cups and two tablespoons sifted flour	2 egg yolks
Pinch of salt	¼ cup light cream
1 cup butter	2 tablespoons white wine

Sift flour and salt together on a kneading board. Rub small pieces of butter with flour between the palms until butter is thoroughly mixed with flour. Make a depression in the middle and in it place the egg yolks, cream and wine. Blend first with a knife, then knead quickly to a smooth dough and keep on kneading until bubbles begin to appear. Put dough in a bowl, cover and refrigerate one hour.

Roll dough on a floured board, fold it over once, then once again crosswise and refrigerate for fifteen minutes. Roll, fold and refrigerate again for fifteen minutes. Repeat again rolling, folding and refrigerating. The dough is now ready to be used in recipes requiring Feuilletage.

Pastries

1 recipe Feuilletage dough I or II

2 tablespoons powdered sugar

2 tablespoons ground chocolate, or

½ pint fresh or well-drained frozen strawberries

1 pint heavy cream, whipped

Roll Feuilletage dough to one-eighth inch thickness and line small muffin pans which have been buttered and floured. Prick bottoms with a fork. Fill with dry navy beans and bake in a moderately hot oven (375 degrees F.) fifteen to twenty minutes or until light brown. Turn the baskets over carefully to spill out the beans. If any beans stick, take them out carefully with fork or spoon. Cool the baskets completely and fill with chocolate or strawberry whipped cream made by folding sugar and chocolate or berries into the whipped cream. Yield: about three dozen baskets.

APPLE CHARLOTTE

1 recipe for Feuilletage dough I or II	9 tablespoons sugar
	6 tablespoons jam
12 medium-size apples	1 egg

Prepare Feuilletage dough and chill in refrigerator. Peel, core and slice apples, sprinkle with four table-spoons sugar and simmer, stirring often, till all liquid has evaporated and apples are thoroughly cooked. Add jam and let it come to a boil while stirring. Cool completely. Divide dough in half and roll one part about one-eighth inch thick to fit a 10 x 15-inch baking pan. Be careful not to break dough in moving it from board to baking pan. The best method is to roll the dough over the rolling pin, lift it and unroll it into the pan.

Spread apple filling on top, leaving bare a margin three-fourths inch wide on all sides. Brush margin with beaten egg. Now roll the second half of dough as the first and carefully place it on top of filling. Press the edges lightly together on all four sides to seal in apples.

Make a few light cuts on top of the charlotte, brush top with beaten egg leaving an unbrushed margin of about one-fourth inch on all four sides. Bake in a moderate oven (375 degrees F.) about twenty minutes. Remove, sprinkle the remaining five tablespoons of sugar on top, return to oven and bake until the charlotte begins to brown. Cut into slices and serve hot or cold. Yield: about thirty slices.

POMME EN ROBE
(APPLE DUMPLINGS)

1 recipe Feuilletage dough I or II	2 eggs
15 medium-sized apples	5 tablespoons powdered sugar
1 cup seedless raisins	

Prepare Feuilletage dough and roll half of it to about one-eighth inch thick. Peel and core apples. Cut dough into squares sufficiently large to envelope an apple. Place an apple in center of each square and fill cavities with raisins. Lift the four corners of dough above the apple and then press corners together. Brush with beaten eggs leaving dry a margin of about one-eighth inch. Repeat, using the second half of the dough. Place apples on a wetted pan and bake in a moderately hot oven (375 degrees F.) about thirty-five or forty minutes. Remove carefully with spatula and sprinkle generously with powdered sugar. Yield: fifteen dumplings.

CRÈME SLICES

~~~~~~

1 recipe Feuilletage
   dough I or II
2 tablespoons flour
¾ cup sugar

6 eggs, separated
1 cup heavy cream
1 egg

Prepare Feuilletage dough and chill in refrigerator. Sift flour and sugar together into double boiler. Add egg yolks one by one, mixing until smooth. Add cream. Cook, beating constantly, until mixture thickens. Cool completely and fold in stiffly beaten egg whites.

Roll dough and fill as Apple Charlotte (page 76) substituting the cooled crème for the apples. Cut, brush with egg and bake as the Apple Charlotte. Yield: about thirty slices.

FEUILLETAGE CRESCENTS

~~~~~~

1 recipe Feuilletage dough I or II
¾ cup jam

1 egg

Roll half of the Feuilletage dough to one-eighth inch thickness and cut into two and one-half inch squares. Keep remainder of dough refrigerated. Place one teaspoonful of jam in center of each square, lift one corner and fold a little toward center. Then roll and bend to form a crescent. Place on a wetted baking pan, spacing crescents about one inch apart, brush with beaten egg and bake in a moderately hot oven (375 degrees F.) about twenty-five minutes. Yield: about three dozen crescents.

Variation: Use Nut Filling (page 25) instead of jam.

FRENCH CHEESE STICKS

~~~~~~

1 recipe Feuilletage dough I or II	¾ cup grated Parmesan or Swiss cheese
1 egg	

Roll Feuilletage dough one-eighth inch thick and cut into strips one inch wide and six inches long. Brush with beaten egg leaving an unbrushed margin about one-eighth inch wide around edges. Cover half of each strip with grated cheese, fold over other half and press edges together. Repeat covering and closing all strips. Place on wetted pan, brush tops with beaten egg leaving a one-eighth inch margin dry along the edges. Bake in a moderately hot oven (375 degrees F.) twenty to twenty-five minutes. Serve sticks while warm. Yield: three and one-half to four dozen sticks.

FEUILLETAGE STICKS

Roll Feuilletage dough I or II to one-eighth inch thickness and cut into sticks one by two and one-half inches. Place on wetted pans and bake in a moderately hot oven (375 degrees F.) twenty to twenty-five minutes. Cool completely and cover with Lemon Icing (page 136) or Chocolate Icing (page 83 or 132).

VOL AU VENT

1 recipe Feuilletage	¾ cup jam, or
dough I or II	½ pint heavy cream,
2 eggs	whipped

Divide Feuilletage dough in half. Place one part in the refrigerator and roll the other part one-fourth inch thick. Cut rounds about two and one-half inches in diameter and place on a wetted pan. Brush with beaten egg leaving a dry margin of about one-eighth inch in width on circumference. Roll second part of dough, and cut rounds about two inches in diameter so that they will be smaller than the first ones. With a tiny cookie cutter, about the size of a thimble, cut out centers of the smaller cookies or use a doughnut cutter for the smaller rounds.

Place the doughnut shapes on top of the larger cookies and brush tops with beaten egg, leaving an uncoated margin of about one-eighth inch around the inner and outer rims of circles so the dough will puff well. Place the small centers on the wetted pan. Bake in a moderately hot oven (375 degrees F.) about twenty-five minutes or until light brown. Remove from the pan carefully with a spatula, allow to cool and fill the centers with jam or whipped cream. Top with the small centers. Yield: one and one-half dozen pastries.

Variation: Fill these Vol au Vents with sea food or chicken salads or with creamed mixtures.

BRANDTEIG KRAPFEN
(CREAM PUFFS)

7 tablespoons shortening
½ cup milk
½ cup water
Pinch of salt
1 cup sifted flour

5 eggs
1 pint heavy cream, whipped
2 tablespoons powdered sugar

Bring to a boil shortening, milk, water and salt. Add flour, reduce heat and continue stirring till batter no longer sticks to the pan. Remove from heat, add eggs, one by one, while beating. Continue beating until a firm batter is formed. Drop by tablespoons on a buttered cookie sheet. Bake in a hot oven (450 degrees F.) about fifteen minutes or until light brown and firm to the touch. Cool, cut top from each puff, remove moist center, fill with whipped cream and replace top. Sprinkle with powdered sugar. Yield: approximately two dozen krapfen.

VIENNA CREAM PUFFS

6 eggs, separated
6 tablespoons sugar
¾ cup sifted flour
½ teaspoon baking
powder
1 tablespoon lemon
juice

Grated rind of one lemon
½ pint heavy cream,
whipped
1 tablespoon powdered
sugar

Beat egg whites stiffly, blend in lightly and quickly sugar, egg yolks, flour sifted with baking powder, lemon juice and rind. Pour batter into small-sized buttered and floured muffin pans, half-filling them. Bake in a slow oven (300 degrees F.) about twenty-five minutes. Take out of pans, trim the crust from around the sides, split each muffin in half and scoop out a small amount of center from both halves. Frost the top halves with chocolate icing. When ready to serve, mix the whipped cream with powdered sugar and fill all the halves. Then pair them, placing the chocolate covered halves on top. Yield: eighteen cream puffs.

Chocolate Icing

1 cup water   2 squares sweet chocolate
⅓ cup sugar

Boil water and sugar. Melt the chocolate in a saucepan and add the sugar syrup while stirring. Cook until
icing is smooth and blended. Use immediately.

LATTICED SLICES

2 cups sifted flour   Grated rind of one-half
Pinch of salt   lemon
⅔ cup butter   1 tablespoon cream
½ cup sugar   2 eggs
½ teaspoon cinnamon   ½ cup jam

Sift flour and salt onto a kneading board. Cut small
pieces of butter into flour. Add sugar, then make a depression in middle of pile and add cinnamon, lemon
rind, cream and one egg. Knead till dough is smooth.
Take about two-thirds of the dough and roll it to fit an
8 x 13-inch pan and cover with jam. Roll remainder of
dough, cut into strips and place as a lattice on top. Beat
remaining egg and brush lattice with it. Bake in a moderate oven (350 degrees F.) about twenty-five or thirty

minutes. When done cut into slices. Yield: about twenty-four slices.

LINZER SQUARES

1¼ cups sweet butter
1½ cups sugar
10 hard-cooked egg yolks, sieved
3 cups sifted flour

1 teaspoon baking powder
1¼ cups almonds
Rind of one lemon, grated
¼ cup currant jelly or plum or raspberry jam

Cream butter and add sugar. Add egg yolks and cream well. Sift together flour and baking powder, add and knead. Slice almonds thinly, or chop finely and add with lemon rind. Knead dough until smooth, then cut off one third. Take larger part and roll to fit a 10 x 15-inch pan. Place dough in pan and cover with jelly or jam. Roll the second batch and cut into strips to form a lattice top. If a sheen is desired, brush lattice lightly with beaten raw egg. Bake in a hot oven (400 degrees F.) about half-an-hour and when cooled cut into two-inch squares. Yield: about four dozen squares.

CHAPTER FIVE

PUDDINGS AND SAUCES

BURNT ALMOND PUDDING

1⅓ cups sugar
1 cup blanched almonds
8 eggs, separated

2 tablespoons lemon juice
Pinch of ground cloves

Heat two-thirds cup sugar slowly in a heavy saucepan, stirring until sugar is browned. Add almonds and stir until almonds are slightly browned, being careful not to burn them. Pour quickly onto a wetted board and let cool. When thoroughly cooled chop mixture finely.

Cream egg yolks with remainder of sugar for fifteen minutes by hand or in electric mixer till thick. Add prepared almonds, lemon juice and cloves and mix well, for twenty minutes, if by hand. Beat egg white stiffly, fold into almond mixture and pour into a well-buttered and floured pudding mold. Cover tightly and steam for forty-five minutes. Turn pudding out and serve with Orange Sauce (page 102). Yield: six to eight servings.

Puddings and Sauces

APPLE PUDDING I

8 eggs, separated
¾ cup sugar
1 cup sifted flour
2 large apples

⅓ cup jam
1 tablespoon powdered
sugar

Add egg yolks, one by one, to sugar and mix for about twenty minutes by hand or in electric mixer till thick. Beat whites of eggs stiffly and fold into mixture. Then add sifted flour. Peel apples, core and cut into rings. Arrange apple rings in bottom of a buttered spring form and fill cavities with jam. Pour egg mixture on top and bake about forty-five minutes in a slow oven (300 degrees F.). When done remove rim of spring form, place pudding upside down on a serving plate, remove bottom of form and sprinkle pudding with powdered sugar. Yield: eight servings.

APPLE PUDDING II

3 medium-sized apples
½ cup white wine
½ cup cold water
1½ cups sugar

⅔ cup sweet butter
6 eggs, separated
½ cup cracker meal

Peel, core and dice apples into saucepan. Add wine, water and half the sugar. Cover and cook over low heat until apples are tender. Cool. Cream butter, add remaining sugar and the egg yolks, one by one. Beat whites of eggs stiffly and fold into creamed mixture. Blend in cracker meal.

Butter and flour a cake or pudding form and cover bottom with a thin layer of batter. Place a layer of stewed apples on top of batter and keep on alternating with layers of batter and stewed apples until mixtures have been used. Bake in a moderate oven (350 degrees F.) about thirty minutes. Yield: six to eight servings.

APPLE OR PEAR COMPOTE AU GELÉE

10 medium-sized apples or pears	¾ cup sugar
	½ cup white wine
5 tablespoons lemon juice	Rind of one-half lemon
	1 teaspoon cinnamon
4 cups water	½ cup currant jelly

Halve apples or pears, core, peel and rub immediately with four tablespoons lemon juice. Place them in two cups of cold water to prevent darkening. To the remaining two cups of water add remaining tablespoon of lemon juice, sugar and wine. Add fruit, cover and simmer until tender but still firm. Take fruit out carefully, arrange in a deep dish, cover and let cool. To juice in which fruit was cooked add lemon rind and cinnamon and cook until mixture begins to thicken. Strain through a fine sieve or muslin cloth into another dish, cool, then place in refrigerator to jell.

To serve, arrange a ring of fruit in a compote dish, add the juice which was drained from it and dress with the chilled jelly and the currant jelly. Yield: ten servings.

APRICOT OR PEACH COMPOTE AU GELÉE

2 tablespoons lemon juice
4 cups water
15 large or twenty small fresh apricots or peaches

¾ cup sugar
Rind of one-half lemon
½ cup currant jelly

Pour half the lemon juice into two cups cold water. Wash fruit, halve, remove stones and place in this acidulated water. Let stand about five minutes while boiling remaining two cups of water with sugar and remaining lemon juice. Add apricots or peaches and simmer till just tender.

Proceed as for Apple Compote Au Gelée (above). Yield: eight servings.

BISCUIT PUDDING AU RHUM

5 tablespoons sweet butter	4 hard-cooked egg
½ cup sugar	yolks
6 egg yolks	4 egg whites
½ cup almonds, ground	⅓ cup rum
2 tablespoons milk	25 lady fingers

Cream butter, sugar and egg yolks thoroughly. Mix almonds with milk. Pass hard-cooked egg yolks through a sieve, blend with almond mixture and add to creamed mixture, blending well. Beat whites of eggs stiffly and fold in. Butter a pudding mold and sprinkle lightly with cracker meal. Pour in about one inch of the pudding mixture, dip some of the lady fingers in rum and arrange on top. Continue alternating pudding mixture with lady fingers dipped in rum, having top layer of pudding mixture. Cover and steam about one hour. Serve with hot Chaudeau (page 101). Yield: ten servings.

BLANCMANGE

1 cup blanched al-
monds, ground
1 pint heavy cream

¾ cup sugar
1 tablespoon cornstarch
12 egg yolks

Mix almonds and cream in a saucepan, heat slowly, stirring, until mixture comes to a boil. Remove from heat, pass through a sieve and let cool. Mix sugar with cornstarch and add egg yolks, one by one. Add gradually to almond mixture beating continuously with an egg beater. When thoroughly blended and foamy, pour into a buttered and floured pudding form and steam forty-five minutes. Serve with thinned jam or Coffee Sauce (page 101). To thin jam add a little water and heat while stirring. Yield: eight servings.

CHESTNUT CROQUETTES

24 cooked chestnuts,
shelled and skinned
¼ cup sweet butter
⅓ cup sugar
2 tablespoons heavy cream

Pinch of salt
3 egg yolks
1 egg
½ cup cracker meal
½ cup shortening

Cut twelve chestnuts in halves and reserve. Pass the remaining twelve chestnuts through a sieve or mash well. Put in double boiler, add butter, sugar, cream, salt and cook, stirring, until mixture thickens. Cool. Mix in egg yolks gradually and place mixture on a floured board. Cut pieces of the chestnut paste sufficiently large to envelope the halved chestnuts and wrap each half in the paste. Dip each croquette in beaten egg, roll in cracker meal and fry in hot fat. Drain on absorbent paper and serve sprinkled with powdered sugar. Yield: six to eight servings.

Cooking Chestnuts

Method I: Shell chestnuts, boil about ten minutes, drain and take off skins. Boil again until chestnuts are soft, yet firm, and drain.

Method II: Make a slit in bottom of each chestnut, cover with cold water and boil covered, for about thirty minutes. Drain and remove shells and skins.

CHESTNUT PURÉE

2 pounds chestnuts
½ cup sugar
2 tablespoons ground sweet chocolate

1 pint heavy cream

Cook chestnuts (page 92) and pass through a sieve or grinder, stir in sugar and chocolate and form a ring on a large platter. Whip cream and place in middle of ring.

If desired serve the purée on individual plates topped with whipped cream. Yield: eight to ten servings.

CHESTNUT PUDDING

¾ pound chestnuts
4 tablespoons sweet butter
¼ cup sifted flour
3 egg yolks
3 eggs
⅓ cup sugar
⅓ cup seedless raisins
6 macaroons, crushed

½ cup bone marrow, diced
10 dates, stoned and diced
5 walnuts, chopped
4 tablespoons rum
4 tablespoons heavy cream

Boil chestnuts (above) and pass one-half through a sieve, or mash well. Add butter, which has been creamed, the flour, egg yolks, eggs, sugar, raisins, macaroons, marrow, dates, walnuts, rum and cream. Blend thoroughly, then dice remaining chestnuts and add to mixture. Pour into a buttered and floured pudding form, cover tightly and steam one hour. Yield: six to eight servings.

CHOCOLATE PUDDING

6 ounces sweet chocolate   3 tablespoons sugar
1/2 cup sweet butter   1/2 pint heavy cream,
4 eggs, separated   whipped
1 teaspoon vanilla

Melt chocolate in a double boiler. Remove from hot water and add butter gradually in small amounts, stirring, until all the butter has been added. Add egg yolks, one by one, blending after each addition, then add vanilla. Continue stirring for about fifteen minutes. Fold in stiffly beaten egg whites and sugar. Pour into a buttered pudding form and chill in refrigerator. Dress with whipped cream before serving. Yield: six servings.

DATE PUDDING

4 slices white bread   3/4 cup sugar
1 cup milk   1/2 cup almonds, chopped
1/2 cup sweet butter   6 ounces dates, diced
8 eggs, separated

Remove crusts and simmer bread in milk until mushy. Remove from heat, add butter and cool. Cream egg yolks with sugar for thirty minutes by hand or beat till thick in electric mixer. Add to first mixture and mix well.

Beat egg whites stiffly and fold in. Mix in lightly the almonds and dates. Turn into a buttered and floured pudding form and steam one hour. If desired, serve with Chocolate Sauce (page 101). Yield: eight servings.

HUNGARIAN RICE PUDDING

1⅔ cups rice	3 tablespoons hot water
4 cups milk	Juice of one orange
½ teaspoon salt	Juice of one lemon
1 tablespoon butter	2 tablespoons rum
¾ cup sugar	½ cup jam or preserves

Wash rice, add to boiling milk, add salt, cover and simmer till tender. Place butter and sugar in a saucepan and brown lightly. Add hot water, orange and lemon juice and bring to a boil. Pour mixture into cooked rice and simmer a couple of minutes. Remove from heat and add rum. Cool.

Spread one layer of rice on a buttered heat-proof platter. Cover rice with a thin layer of warm jam or preserves, then follow with alternate layers of rice and jam until all ingredients have been used. Spread meringue evenly over top and sides of pudding and bake in a slow oven (325 degrees F.) ten to fifteen minutes or until meringue is lightly browned. Yield: six to eight servings.

Meringue

~~~~~~

3 egg whites   ½ teaspoon vanilla
⅓ cup sugar

Beat egg whites till foamy. Add sugar gradually and beat till mixture forms stiff peaks. Add vanilla.

FROTH PUDDING

~~~~~~

¾ cup sugar   5 egg whites
½ cup jam   ⅓ cup diced almonds
2 eggs

Place in a mixing bowl sugar, jam and eggs and mix well for about twenty minutes by hand or beat till thick in an electric mixer. Fold in the stiffly beaten egg whites. Pour mixture into a buttered casserole, filling it half-full. Sprinkle almonds on top and bake in a slow oven (300 degrees F.) for one hour. Serve immediately. Yield: six servings.

MARASCHINO PUDDING

⅔ cup sweet butter	1 cup almonds, ground
¾ cup sugar	6 egg whites
10 egg yolks	15 lady fingers,
3 tablespoons mara-	crumbed
schino liqueur	

Cream butter, add sugar, egg yolks, one by one, and maraschino. Mix for fifteen minutes by hand or in electric mixer till thick. Add almonds and mix for another fifteen minutes. Fold in stiffly beaten egg whites and lady fingers. Turn into a buttered and floured pudding mold and steam for forty-five minutes. Yield: eight to ten servings.

ORANGE PUDDING

2 slices white bread	¾ cup sugar
½ cup milk	6 eggs, separated
Juice of one orange	1 cup blanched almonds,
7 tablespoons sweet	ground
butter	

Remove crusts from bread and boil in milk until mushy. Remove from heat, add orange juice and pass mixture through a sieve. Cream butter with sugar, add egg yolks gradually, and add almonds. Add milk mixture. Beat egg whites stiffly and fold in. Turn into a buttered and floured pudding mold, cover and steam for forty-five minutes. Serve with any desired sauce. Yield: six servings.

TURKISH RICE PUDDING

¾ cup rice	½ teaspoon cinnamon
2 cups milk	5 medium-sized apples
4 tablespoons butter	1 recipe of meringue
¾ cup sugar	(above)

Wash rice well, add to boiling milk and cook in double boiler until thick. Cream butter with sugar and add to rice. Add cinnamon and cool. Peel apples, cut into thick slices, and fry in butter until lightly browned on both sides. Place cooked rice in a buttered casserole, make a depression in the center and fill with fried apple slices. Cover with meringue and bake in a slow oven (350 degrees F.) about fifteen minutes or until meringue is lightly browned. Yield: four to six servings.

VIENNESE PUDDING

⅔ cup butter, scant
⅔ cup sugar
⅔ cup blanched almonds, ground

7 egg yolks
4 egg whites

Cream butter and sugar. Add almonds and egg yolks and mix for twenty minutes by hand or in electric mixer till thick. Beat egg whites stiffly and fold into creamed mixture. Pour into a buttered casserole and bake in a moderate oven (350 degrees F.) about thirty minutes. Serve immediately.

If desired, Chaudeau (page 101) may be served as a sauce with this pudding. Yield: six to eight servings.

WHITE PUDDING

〰〰〰〰〰〰〰〰〰〰〰〰〰〰〰〰

2/3 cup sweet butter   1/2 teaspoon cinnamon
3/4 cup sugar   Grated rind of one-half
6 hard-cooked eggs, sieved   lemon
3/4 cup blanched almonds,   6 egg whites
   ground

Cream butter with sugar, add egg yolks, almonds, cinnamon and lemon rind. Fold in stiffly beaten egg whites. Pour into a buttered and floured pudding form and steam thirty minutes. Serve with Almond Sauce (below). Yield: six to eight servings.

ALMOND SAUCE

〰〰〰〰〰〰〰〰〰〰〰〰〰〰〰〰

1/2 cup blanched almonds,   4 egg yolks
   finely chopped   1/2 cup sugar
1 pint heavy cream

Bring almonds and cream to a boil. Cream egg yolks with sugar and add gradually, stirring, to first mixture. Cook, beating constantly with an egg beater until sauce has thickened. Yield: about two and one-half cups.

CHAUDEAU

~~~~~~~~~~~~~~~~~~~~~~~~~~~~~~~~~~~~~~~

6 egg yolks	Juice of one orange
2/3 cup sugar	Juice of one lemon
1/2 cup white wine	

Place egg yolks in a large double boiler and add remaining ingredients. Beat mixture constantly while cooking over simmering water until frothy. Use electric beater if possible. Pour into a serving bowl and serve immediately. Yield: six servings.

Note: Chaudeau may be served as a dessert with cookies.

CHOCOLATE SAUCE

~~~~~~~~~~~~~~~~~~~~~~~~~~~~~~~~~~~~~~~

1/2 cup water	1 pint heavy cream
2/3 cup sugar	4 egg yolks, beaten
4 squares sweet chocolate	

Boil together water and sugar to a light syrup (228 degrees F.). Melt chocolate in a double boiler and add syrup slowly, stirring until smooth. Blend cream and egg yolks and add the chocolate mixture gradually. Return to double boiler and, using a rotary beater, beat continuously, while cooking, until sauce has thickened. Yield: three cups.

COFFEE SAUCE

4 egg yolks	$\frac{1}{2}$ cup very strong coffee
$\frac{2}{3}$ cup sugar	1 pint heavy cream

Cream egg yolks with sugar in a saucepan, add coffee slowly. Then follow with cream. Cook over low heat until thickened, using an egg beater constantly. Yield: about two and three-fourths cups.

ORANGE SAUCE

1 orange, peeled and seeded	1 pint heavy cream
$\frac{2}{3}$ cup sugar	4 egg yolks

Place orange in a bowl with sugar and mash. Add three tablespoons cream and let mixture stand till sugar is dissolved. Place remaining cream, egg yolks and orange mixture in a double boiler and cook, beating constantly, until mixture thickens. Use an electric beater if possible. Yield: about two and one-half cups.

CHAPTER SIX

SOUFFLÉS

ALMOND SOUFFLÉ I

¾ cup sweet butter
¾ cup sugar
10 eggs, separated
1 teaspoon vanilla
1 cup blanched almonds,
  ground

1 egg white
2 sweet rolls
⅓ cup milk

Cream butter, mix in sugar, add egg yolks, one by one, and cream until smooth. Add vanilla. Mix almonds with one egg white. Remove crusts from rolls, soak rolls in milk, then squeeze out excess milk and stir together with almond mixture into batter. Lastly fold in the ten egg whites, stiffly beaten, and pour into a nine-inch deep cake form. Bake in a slow oven (300 degrees F.) about forty minutes. Take out of form and serve warm. Yield: eight servings.

ALMOND SOUFFLÉ II

⅓ cup sifted flour
1 cup light cream
5 tablespoons butter
⅓ cup sugar
7 egg yolks

3 tablespoons blanched
   almonds, sliced
5 egg whites
10 small lady fingers

Place flour in double boiler, add cream slowly and stir so as not to form lumps. Cook, stirring, until mixture thickens and cools. Cream butter and sugar and add egg yolks one by one. Add and blend into cooled mixture. Add sliced almonds and fold in egg whites, stiffly beaten. Pour into a buttered eight-inch deep cake form. Halve the lady fingers, insert into soufflé, letting ends show and arranging as desired. Bake in a slow oven (300 degrees F.) about forty minutes. Serve warm or cold. Yield: eight to ten servings.

APRICOT SOUFFLÉ

3 tablespoons sweet butter
¼ cup apricot jam

⅓ cup sugar
7 eggs, separated

Cream butter and jam, add sugar, egg yolks gradually, and continue mixing for twenty minutes by hand or in an electric mixer till thick. Lastly fold in stiffly beaten whites of eggs. Pour mixture into a well-buttered casserole which has been sprinkled with sugar and bake in a slow oven (300 degrees F.) about thirty minutes. Serve immediately. Yield: six to eight servings.

CHOCOLATE SOUFFLÉ

4 egg yolks	1 cup milk
4 tablespoons sugar	1 tablespoon grated
3 tablespoons sifted flour	chocolate

Cream egg yolks with sugar. Add flour and, while stirring, add the milk slowly. When smooth, pour mixture into a buttered casserole. Bake fifteen minutes in a hot oven (400 degrees F.). Sprinkle with chocolate and serve immediately. Yield: four servings.

SOUFFLÉ À LA CRÈME

⅔ cup sifted flour
¾ cup sugar
2 cups milk
1 teaspoon vanilla

8 eggs, separated
1 tablespoon powdered
sugar

Sift flour into a double boiler and mix in sugar. Add milk slowly and cook until mixture thickens, stirring occasionally. Add vanilla and let mixture cool completely. Add egg yolks, one by one, and then fold in stiffly beaten egg whites. Pour into a buttered and floured casserole and bake in a slow oven (300 degrees F.) about forty minutes. Sprinkle with powdered sugar and serve immediately. Yield: ten to twelve servings.

LEMON SOUFFLÉ

⅓ cup sifted flour
1 cup cream
¾ cup sugar
7 eggs, separated

2 tablespoons lemon
juice
1 tablespoon powdered
sugar

Sift flour into saucepan, add cream gradually and stir continuously over low heat until mixture thickens. Pour batter into a mixing bowl and let it cool. Mix sugar, egg yolks and lemon juice for about twenty minutes by hand or in electric mixer till thick. Then add, slowly, to cooled batter. Beat whites of eggs stiffly and fold in. Pour mixture into a buttered casserole and bake in a slow oven (300 degrees F.) about one hour, or until done. Sprinkle with powdered sugar and serve immediately. Yield: eight servings.

SOUFFLÉ AUX NOIX

¾ cup sweet butter
¾ cup sugar
10 egg yolks
3 cups broken walnuts, ground

1 teaspoon powdered coffee
8 egg whites
½ pint heavy cream

Cream butter well, add sugar, then egg yolks, one by one, and mix until smooth and thick by hand or in an electric mixer. Add walnuts and coffee. Lastly fold in stiffly beaten egg whites. Bake in a buttered and floured nine-inch cake form or casserole for about forty-five minutes in a slow oven (300 degrees F.). Serve hot or cold, covered with whipped cream. Yield: ten to twelve servings.

MERINGUE SOUFFLÉ

~~~~~~

⅓ cup sifted flour	½ cup sugar
1 cup milk	⅓ cup warm jam
6 eggs, separated	

Sift flour into a double boiler. Add milk slowly, stirring to prevent lumps. Cook, stirring, until mixture thickens. Cool, stirring occasionally. Add egg yolks gradually, then add one-third cup sugar and continue mixing for fifteen minutes by hand or in electric mixer till thick. Fold in four stiffly-beaten egg whites, pour into a buttered casserole and bake in a slow oven (300 degrees F.) about forty-five minutes.

Spread the warm jam lightly on top, cover with meringue, and return soufflé to oven for about fifteen minutes. To make meringue, beat whites of two remaining eggs, add remaining one-fourth cup sugar and beat till mixture forms stiff peaks. Yield: eight to ten servings.

RICE SOUFFLÉ

~~~~~~

1 cup rice	8 eggs, separated
2 cups milk	¾ cup sugar
½ cup butter	Powdered sugar
Pinch of salt	

Wash rice and cook in milk until done. Remove from heat, mix in butter and salt and let mixture cool. Cream egg yolks with sugar for thirty minutes by hand or in electric mixer till thick. Add to the cooled rice, then fold in stiffly beaten egg whites. Pour into a deep well-buttered and floured cake form or casserole and bake about forty minutes in a moderate oven (350 degrees F.). Sprinkle with powdered sugar before serving. Yield: eight servings.

RICE SOUFFLÉ WITH APPLES

1 recipe rice soufflé (above)
3 apples

2 tablespoons sugar
Confectioners' sugar

Prepare rice soufflé mixture. When ready to fill cake form use only half the mixture and bake it for ten minutes in a slow oven (300 degrees F.). Pare, core and slice apples thinly and arrange over baked rice mixture. Sprinkle with sugar and cover with rest of rice. Return to oven, raise temperature to moderate (350 degrees F.) and bake for about thirty-five minutes. Sprinkle confectioners' sugar on top before serving. Yield: eight to ten servings.

SNOW SOUFFLÉ

4 egg whites
4 tablespoons sugar
Pinch of salt

1 tablespoon butter
2 tablespoons cherry
brandy

Beat whites of eggs until stiff. Add and mix in sugar and salt. Pour into a buttered casserole. Bake eight minutes in a moderate oven (350 degrees F.). Sprinkle with cherry brandy and serve immediately. Yield: four servings.

CHAPTER SEVEN

SWEET BREADS–QUICK AND YEAST

ALMOND BREAD I

1 cup sugar	Rind of one lemon
2 eggs	1⅔ cups sifted flour
2 egg yolks	1 teaspoon baking
1 cup almonds, chopped	powder

Cream sugar, eggs and egg yolks well. Add almonds and grated lemon rind. Sift together flour and baking powder and add to mixture. Bake in a greased loaf pan for about one hour in a slow oven (300 degrees F.). Cool before slicing. Yield: one loaf bread.

ALMOND BREAD II

1⅔ cups sugar	2⅔ cups sifted flour
14 egg yolks	1 teaspoon baking powder
1 egg	1½ cups almonds

Place sugar in a mixing bowl, blend in egg yolks, one by one, and then add the whole egg. Sift together flour and baking powder, add and blend into egg mixture. Stir in whole almonds. Pour into a well-buttered loaf pan and bake in a moderate oven (350 degrees F.) for about one hour. Cut into one-half inch slices while still hot. Yield: one loaf bread.

FRENCH PANCAKES

1 cup sifted flour	1 tablespoon sparkling water
Pinch of salt	$\frac{1}{3}$ cup melted butter
3 eggs	Jam
1 cup milk	1 tablespoon powdered sugar

Sift flour and salt into a mixing bowl and gradually stir in eggs and milk. Add sparkling water and mix until batter is smooth.

Heat a small frying pan and brush with butter. Pour in two or three tablespoons of batter, or enough to cover pan thinly and evenly. When brown on one side, turn with a spatula and brown other side. If necessary brush pan with butter when turning pancake. Repeat until all the batter has been used, brushing skillet with butter for each pancake and letting the pancakes accumulate on a platter in a warm place. Before serving, spread jam lightly on each pancake, roll and sprinkle with powdered sugar. Yield: about eighteen pancakes.

HUNGARIAN PANCAKES

1 recipe for French Pancakes (above)	1 egg
	1/4 cup light cream
2/3 cup sugar	1/2 pint sour cream
1 pound dry cottage cheese	1 tablespoon sugar
	1 tablespoon cinnamon
1/3 cup seedless raisins	

Bake pancakes and keep warm. Mix sugar with cottage cheese. Add raisins, egg and light cream and mix. Spread small portion of mixture on each pancake, fold in half and then fold again crosswise. Repeat filling and folding of all pancakes.

In the bottom of a buttered casserole arrange four of the filled pancakes with the curved edges toward the outside. Repeat with remaining pancakes. Pour sour cream on top and bake in a slow oven (300 degrees F.) about ten minutes. Mix tablespoon of sugar with cinnamon and sprinkle on top of pancakes before serving. Yield: about eighteen pancakes.

TEA MUFFINS

¾ cup sweet butter   1 scant cup cracker meal
⅔ cup sugar   ½ teaspoon baking powder
8 egg yolks   1 tablespoon powdered
½ teaspoon vanilla   sugar
4 egg whites

Cream butter well, add sugar, then add egg yolks, one by one, and vanilla. Beat whites of eggs stiffly and fold into mixture. Mix cracker meal with baking powder and add gradually. Fill greased muffin pans half-full and bake in a moderate oven (350 degrees F.) twenty-five to thirty minutes. Sprinkle with powdered sugar. Yield: eighteen muffins.

MUFFINS WITH CHAUDEAU

3 tablespoons sweet   1 teaspoon lemon extract
   butter   3 egg whites
⅔ cup sugar   1¼ cups sifted flour
6 egg yolks   1 teaspoon baking powder
3 tablespoons heavy   Chaudeau (page 101)
   cream, whipped

Cream butter, mix in sugar, add egg yolks gradually and cream till smooth. Add whipped cream and lemon extract. Fold in whites of eggs, stiffly beaten, and lastly sift flour with baking powder and blend in. Fill small buttered muffin forms half-full and bake from twenty-five to thirty minutes in a moderate oven (350 degrees F.). Serve with Chaudeau. Yield: eighteen muffins.

BRIOCHE

⅔ cup butter	½ cup lukewarm milk
3 tablespoons sugar	2 cups plus two table-
8 egg yolks	spoons sifted flour
1 egg	½ teaspoon salt
2 packages yeast	Powdered sugar

Cream butter and sugar well and add egg yolks, one by one, and the egg. Dissolve yeast in milk and add to mixture. Combine flour and salt and sift into cream mixture. Mix until dough will not stick to the bowl.

Butter muffin cups, dust with flour and fill only half full. Cover with a cloth and let stand in a warm place (80 to 85 degrees F.) until risen. Bake in a moderately hot oven (375 degrees F.) about thirty-five minutes. Sprinkle with powdered sugar before serving. Yield: about thirty rolls.

BUCHTELN (VIENNESE JAM OR NUT BUNS)

6 tablespoons sweet butter

1 tablespoon sugar

Pinch of salt

2 egg yolks

1 egg

1 package yeast

½ cup lukewarm milk

2 cups plus two tablespoons sifted flour

Jam, or Walnut Filling (page 129)

2 tablespoons melted butter

2 tablespoons powdered sugar

Cream butter, add gradually sugar, salt, egg yolks and egg. Dissolve yeast in lukewarm milk and stir into mixture. Add flour and mix until dough does not stick to bowl. Cover with a cloth and let stand in a warm place (80 to 85 degrees F.) to rise for about one hour.

Then roll on a floured board to one-half inch thickness and cut into pieces about two by three inches. Along the center of each piece spread one teaspoon of jam or the Walnut Filling. Lift a three-inch side, cover filling and roll. Close buns by pressing the ends.

Butter a shallow pan and place buns close enough to touch, having first brushed melted butter in between. Buchtelns are always placed in pan with their flaps up. When the pan is filled, cover with a cloth and let stand in a warm place (80 to 85 degrees F.) to rise till twice their size. Bake in a moderate oven (350 degrees F.) about forty-five minutes. Separate the buns and sprinkle with powdered sugar. Serve warm or cold. Yield: about thirty Buchtelns.

ALICE'S BUTTER SLICES

2¼ cups sifted flour
1 cup sweet butter, softened
3 eggs, separated
1 tablespoon sugar
1 package yeast

¼ cup milk
1 cup jam
½ cup ground walnuts, mixed with 1 tablespoon sugar

Sift flour into mixing bowl. Add butter, egg yolks and sugar and knead until smooth. Add yeast, dissolved in milk, and resume kneading for about five minutes or until dough is no longer sticky. Leave dough in bowl, cover with a cloth and let stand in a warm place (80 to 85 degrees F.) for two hours or until double in bulk.

Then divide dough into three equal parts and roll each part separately to fit an 8 x 13-inch pan. Cover bottom layer with jam and sprinkle with one-third of the ground walnuts and sugar. Place second layer on top and use same filling of jam and walnuts. Top with third layer, brush lightly with egg white and sprinkle with remaining walnut and sugar mixture. Bake in a moderate oven (350 degrees F.) about thirty minutes. Cool in pan and slice as desired. Yield: twenty to twenty-four slices.

COFFEE CAKE

1 package yeast
1½ cups lukewarm milk
½ cup sugar
3¾ cups sifted flour
7 tablespoons butter, melted

2 eggs
¼ teaspoon salt
½ cup seedless
  raisins

Dissolve yeast in half the milk, add one tablespoon sugar and one tablespoon flour and stir till smooth. Pour remainder of milk into mixing bowl, add cooled butter, rest of sugar and eggs. Sift flour and salt together and add alternately the yeast and milk mixtures. Knead dough until it blisters and then knead in raisins. Brush surface with melted fat, cover with cloth and let rise in a warm place (80 to 85 degrees F.) for about two hours or till double in bulk.

Shape and place in any desired type of greased cake form, filling it not over one-half full. Let it stand covered in a warm place (80 to 85 degrees F.) till almost double in bulk. Then bake in a moderate oven (375 degrees F.) about one hour. If cake browns too fast, reduce heat to low (325 degrees F.) after first thirty minutes. Yield: one very large loaf.

FRENCH CRESCENTS

1½ packages yeast
1½ cups lukewarm milk
3¾ cups sifted flour
¼ teaspoon salt

½ cup butter, melted
2 eggs
2 tablespoons sugar

Dissolve yeast in lukewarm milk and add gradually to flour that has been sifted with salt. Add cooled butter, eggs and sugar. Knead until dough is smooth and does not stick to the hands. If necessary sprinkle hands with flour while kneading. Cover dough with a cloth and let stand in a warm place (80 to 85 degrees F.) for about one hour. Knead again for a few minutes, cover and let rise again in a warm place for another hour.

Then roll dough on a floured board to about one-fourth inch thickness, cut into three to four-inch squares and place in the center of each one teaspoonful of either Walnut Filling (page 129), cheese filling (below), or

[**119**]

jam. Lift one corner and fold toward center and on top of filling, then roll and bend to form a crescent. Place on a buttered shallow pan, cover with a cloth and let rise again in a warm place for about fifteen minutes. If a sheen is desired brush with one beaten egg just before placing in oven, and bake in a moderately hot oven (375 degrees F.) about thirty-five minutes. Yield: about three dozen crescents.

Cheese Filling

1 pound dry cottage cheese	2 tablespoons butter
	1/2 cup sugar
2 egg yolks	1/2 cup sultana raisins

Mix all ingredients.

BISCUIT GUGELHUPF
(*Select Coffee Cake*)

1 cup butter	1/4 cup milk
3 tablespoons sugar	6 egg whites, beaten
Pinch of salt	2 cups plus two table-
12 egg yolks	spoons sifted flour
1 1/2 packages yeast	1/3 cup almonds, shaved

Cream butter, add gradually sugar, salt and egg yolks. Dissolve yeast in milk and add to mixture. Fold in egg whites and then flour, folding lightly until all ingredients are blended.

Butter a slightly warmed pudding form, sprinkle with the shaved almonds and fill somewhat less than half-full. Cover with a cloth and stand in a warm place (80 to 85 degrees F.) until dough has doubled in volume.

Then bake in a moderately hot oven (375 degrees F.) for twenty minutes. Reduce temperature to low (325 degrees F.) and bake about thirty minutes longer. Cool on a cake rack and ice as desired, or sprinkle with powdered sugar. Yield: one loaf.

FIVE O'CLOCK GUGELHUPF

2 cups and two tablespoons sifted flour	1 egg
Pinch of salt	1 package yeast
⅔ cup butter	½ cup lukewarm milk
2 tablespoons sugar	Grated rind of one-half lemon
1 teaspoon vanilla	⅓ cup seedless raisins
3 egg yolks	

Sift flour and salt together on a kneading board. Rub flour with small pieces of butter between palms and when well mixed place in bowl. Add gradually, sugar, vanilla, egg yolks, one by one, and the egg. Dissolve yeast in milk, add to flour mixture together with lemon rind and mix until dough no longer sticks to bowl. Lastly add raisins and place dough in a well-buttered pudding mold, leaving sufficient space for it to double its volume.

Cover with a cloth and let stand in a warm place (80 to 85 degrees F.) until it has doubled in size. Then bake in a moderately hot oven (375 degrees F.) thirty minutes. Reduce temperature to moderate (350 degrees F.) and bake about fifteen minutes more or until gugelhupf is done. Yield: one loaf.

SWISS GUGELHUPF

⅔ cup butter	2 cups plus two table-
5 egg yolks	spoons sifted flour
2 tablespoons sugar	Pinch of salt
1 package yeast	1 egg white
½ cup lukewarm milk, approximately	⅓ cup seedless raisins

Cream butter well and add gradually egg yolks and sugar. Dissolve yeast in one-quarter cup milk. Sift flour and salt together and add alternately with yeast to creamed mixture. Use enough additional milk to give a soft dough. Work until mixture no longer sticks to the bowl. Blend in the stiffly beaten egg white and add raisins.

Fill a pudding mold half full, let rise till doubled in volume and bake in a moderately hot oven (375 degrees F.) thirty minutes. Reduce temperature to moderate (350 degrees F.) and bake about fifteen minutes longer. Swiss Gugelhupf is not iced. Yield: one loaf.

VIENNESE GUGELHUPF

⅔ cup sweet butter   3 cups flour
2 tablespoons sugar   Pinch of salt
5 egg yolks   ⅓ cup jam
2 packages yeast   1 egg
½ cup lukewarm milk   ¼ cup shaved almonds

Cream butter, add one tablespoon sugar and mix in the egg yolks, one by one. Dissolve yeast in milk and add. Sift flour and salt together, add and mix until dough no longer sticks to bowl. Cover and let rise in a warm place (80 to 85 degrees F.) about thirty or forty minutes. Then place dough on a floured board and divide in two equal parts.

Roll one-half to fit a deep well-buttered and floured

cake form, spread jam on top leaving uncovered about one-half inch margin around edge and brush this margin with beaten egg. Roll second part of dough and place on top, press edges lightly together, cover with a cloth and let rise again for about thirty minutes in a warm place (80 to 85 degrees F.) Then brush top with beaten egg, sprinkle with almonds and the remaining one tablespoon sugar and bake in a moderately hot oven (375 degrees F.) about twenty minutes. Reduce temperature to low (325 degrees F.) and bake about thirty minutes longer. Yield: one large loaf.

JAM BASKETS

½ cup butter	½ cup lukewarm light cream
⅓ cup sugar	2½ cups sifted flour
2 egg yolks	¼ teaspoon salt
1 egg	½ cup jam
1½ packages yeast	⅓ cup chopped almonds

Cream butter and add gradually sugar, egg yolks and egg. Dissolve yeast in cream and add to mixture. Add flour and salt and mix until dough no longer sticks to bowl. Cover mixing bowl with a cloth and let stand in a warm place (80 to 85 degrees F.) to rise till double in bulk. Then place on a floured board and roll to about one-eighth-inch thickness. Cut into three-inch squares and put about one-half teaspoon jam in the center of each square. Lift corners, bring them together toward center and press points and edges together to form a basket.

Place baskets on buttered cookie sheets, cover lightly and let stand in a warm place for about twenty minutes. Sprinkle with chopped almond and bake in a moderately hot oven (375 degrees F.) about thirty minutes. Yield: about three dozen baskets.

FIVE O'CLOCK SLICES

⅔ cup sweet butter	1¼ cups sifted flour
3 egg yolks	⅓ cup chopped walnuts
2 eggs	2 tablespoons sugar
1½ packages yeast	1 teaspoon cinnamon
¼ cup lukewarm milk	

Cream butter, add egg yolks, one egg and yeast which has been dissolved in milk. Add flour and mix until dough no longer sticks to spoon or hand. Roll this about one-half inch thick and fit into a buttered pan, cover with cloth and let stand in a warm place (80 to 85 degrees F.) about one hour or until dough has doubled in bulk. Then beat remaining egg and brush over top. Sprinkle with mixture of walnuts, sugar and cinnamon and bake in a moderately hot oven (375 degrees F.) about forty minutes. Cut into slices one by three inches and serve either warm or cold with tea, coffee or chocolate. Yield: two and one-half to three dozen slices.

SNOW CAKE

⅔ cup butter	3 egg whites
¼ cup sugar	1 tablespoon melted
Pinch of salt	butter
2 packages yeast	Cheese Spread
½ cup heavy cream	Walnut Spread
3 cups sifted flour	⅓ cup jam

Cream butter with sugar and salt. Dissolve yeast in lukewarm cream and add to creamed mixture. Add flour, and mix until dough no longer sticks to the bowl. Blend in stiffly beaten egg whites. Place dough on a floured board and roll to about one-half-inch thickness. Cut into four rounds about the size of a dinner plate. Pinch the margin of each layer and raise it so that the edge will stand up a little. Set the four rounds in a warm place (80 to 85 degrees F.), cover with a cloth and let rise till double in thickness. Then place them in buttered pans, cover two rounds with Cheese Spread and one with jam. Brush the fourth lightly with melted butter and cover with Walnut Spread. Bake in a moderate oven (350 degrees F.) about thirty minutes. Place the jam covered layer between the two cheese layers and top with the walnut-covered layer. Cut into slices and serve hot or cold. Yield: one large loaf.

Cheese Spread

½ pound dry cottage cheese

2 tablespoons sugar

Grated rind one-half lemon

¼ cup sultana raisins

Mix all ingredients thoroughly.

Walnut Spread

⅓ cup chopped walnuts

2 tablespoons sugar

1 teaspoon cinnamon

Mix ingredients well.

WALNUT COFFEE ROLL

2⅔ cups sifted flour
¼ teaspoon salt
1 package yeast
1 cup lukewarm milk

3 tablespoons butter, melted
1 egg yolk
1 egg

Sift flour and salt into a mixing bowl. Dissolve yeast in lukewarm milk and add. Cool butter and add. Add the egg yolk and knead until dough is smooth, cover with a cloth and let rise in a warm place (80 to 85 degrees F.) about two hours or till double in bulk. Remove dough to a floured board and roll to about one-fourth inch thickness. Cover completely with Walnut Filling and roll as a jelly roll. Place on a well-buttered shallow pan and let stand in a warm place fifteen minutes. Brush roll with beaten egg and bake in a moderately hot oven (375 degrees F.) about forty-five minutes, reduce temperature to low (300 degrees F.) and bake about fifteen minutes longer. Cool on a cake rack. Yield: ten servings.

Walnut Filling

¾ cup sugar   2 cups walnuts, ground
1 cup cold water   ½ cup seedless raisins
1 teaspoon vanilla   or sultanas

Place sugar, water and vanilla in a saucepan and cook over low heat until syrupy (232 degrees F.). Mix walnuts and raisins and add to the hot syrup. Cool before using.

CHAPTER EIGHT

TORTES

ALCAZAR TORTE

~~~~~~

6 egg whites	½ cup jam
1 cup sugar	1 pint heavy cream,
2 cups broken	whipped
walnuts, ground	Ground chocolate, optional

Beat egg whites stiffly, add sugar and then fold in ground walnuts. Bake in four well-buttered layer pans about fifteen minutes in a moderate oven (350 degrees F.). Cool, spread jam on first layer, place next layer on top and spread with whipped cream. Alternate spreads of jam and whipped cream on the remaining two layers. Cover sides of torte with whipped cream. If desired, sprinkle with ground chocolate. Yield: twelve or more servings.

TORTE À L'ALLIANCE I

~~~~~~

4 tablespoons sweet
butter
½ cup sugar
6 eggs, separated
1 teaspoon vanilla

½ cup almonds, ground
3 tablespoons ground
sweet chocolate
2 tablespoons powdered
sugar

Cream butter and sugar, add egg yolks, one by one, and vanilla. Mix for fifteen minutes by hand or in an electric mixer till thick. Fold in almonds. Beat egg whites stiffly, fold in and then fold in chocolate. Pour into a deep buttered and floured cake form and bake in a moderate oven (350 degrees F.) about thirty minutes. Cool on a cake rack and sprinkle with powdered sugar. Yield: ten or more servings.

TORTE À L'ALLIANCE II

~~~~~~

⅓ cup sugar
4 eggs, separated
6 tablespoons sweet butter,
melted

⅔ cup sifted flour
⅓ cup jam

Cream sugar with egg yolks for fifteen minutes by hand or in electric mixer. Add alternately tablespoons of butter and tablespoons of flour. Fold in stiffly beaten whites of eggs. Pour into a deep buttered and floured cake form and bake in a moderate oven (350 degrees F.) thirty minutes. Cool on a cake rack, spread a thin layer of warm jam on top and cover with Chocolate Icing. Yield: eight servings.

Chocolate Icing

Melt four ounces of sweet chocolate and mix with four tablespoons of light cream.

ALMOND TORTE (UNCOOKED)
Mixture I

1 cup plus two table-	9 ounces sweet chocolate,
spoons sweet butter	melted
1¼ cups sugar	1 teaspoon vanilla

Cream butter and sugar. Mix chocolate and vanilla and blend gradually into butter and sugar mixture. Line a deep cake form with waxed paper, fill with mixture and place in refrigerator to chill.

Tortes

Mixture II

1 cup plus two table-
  spoons sweet butter
1¼ cups sugar

1⅔ cups blanched
  almonds, ground
3 tablespoons light cream

Cream butter with sugar, add almonds and mix in cream. Place this mixture on top of the well-chilled Mixture I and return to refrigerator. When torte is thoroughly chilled cover with Chocolate Icing (above), and return to refrigerator until ready to serve. Yield: twelve servings.

FRENCH ALMOND TORTE
Mixture I

4 egg whites
⅔ cup water
1 cup almonds,
  ground

½ teaspoon baking powder
4 ounces sweet chocolate,
  ground
1 teaspoon vanilla

Beat egg whites, add sugar and beat until stiff. Add almonds, baking powder, chocolate and vanilla. Bake in a buttered cake form about thirty-five minutes in a moderate oven (350 degrees F.).

Mixture II

~~~~~~

3 egg whites
2/3 cup sugar
1 cup blanched almonds,
   ground

1/2 teaspoon baking
   powder
1 teaspoon vanilla

Combine ingredients as for Mixture I but bake about ten minutes longer. Spread the following filling between the two layers and cover the torte with it. It is advisable to bake the layers the day before they are to be filled. If desired, sprinkle ground almonds over top of torte. Yield: twelve or more servings.

Chocolate Butter Filling

~~~~~~

3/4 cup sweet butter
2 tablespoons sugar
3 heaping tablespoons
   ground sweet chocolate

1/2 teaspoon vanilla

Cream butter and sugar, add chocolate and vanilla and cream until smooth.

Tortes

TORTE BAVAROISE

1 cup blanched almonds, ground
1 egg white
1⅓ cups sweet butter, creamed
Juice of one lemon
¾ cup sugar
1 teaspoon vanilla
6 hard-cooked egg yolks
2¾ cups sifted flour
1 teaspoon baking powder
½ cup jam or preserves

Mix almonds and white of egg and add to creamed butter. Mix in lemon juice, sugar and vanilla. Sieve hard-cooked egg yolks and add. Sift together flour and baking powder, add and knead until dough is smooth. Divide dough into thirds, roll to fit, and place in three layer-cake pans which have been lined with buttered waxed paper. Bake about thirty minutes in a moderate oven (350 degrees F.). Cool torte completely, spread jam between layers and cover with Lemon icing (page 136). Yield: ten to twelve servings.

BISCUIT TORTE

¾ cup sugar
1 teaspoon vanilla
4 eggs
4 egg yolks
½ teaspoon cornstarch
1 cup sifted flour
½ teaspoon baking powder

Place all ingredients except flour and baking powder in a double boiler. Cook, beating constantly, until mixture thickens. Remove from heat and continue beating until cooled.

Sift together flour and baking powder and blend into custard. Bake in a deep buttered spring form for about one hour in a slow oven (250 degrees F.). Cool and cover with Lemon or Orange Icing. Yield: eight servings.

Lemon Icing

2 cups confectioners' sugar	1 teaspoon sweet butter, or
5 tablespoons lemon juice	1 tablespoon light cream

Mix confectioners' sugar and lemon juice until smooth, then add the butter or cream and mix well. Thin icing with a little cream if it is too thick, or add a little more sugar if it is too thin.

Orange Icing

Use above recipe and substitute orange juice for lemon juice.

Tortes

TORTE À LA BRABANTE

~~~~~~

1⅓ cups sifted flour	⅓ cup sugar
1 teaspoon baking powder	½ teaspoon
¾ cup sweet butter	cinnamon
½ cup almonds, ground	½ cup jam

Sift flour and baking powder together onto a kneading board. Cut butter into flour, add almonds and mix. Sift together sugar and cinnamon, add to dough and knead till smooth. Cut into three parts, roll to fit and place in three layer pans. Bake for about thirty minutes in a moderate oven (350 degrees F.). Cool layers, and remove carefully from pans. Spread jam between layers and cover torte with Lemon Icing (page 136). Yield: ten servings.

BUTTER TORTE I

~~~~~~

2¾ cups sifted flour	⅔ cup sugar
1 teaspoon baking powder	½ cup jam
¾ cup sweet butter	1 tablespoon confectioners' sugar

Sift together flour and baking powder. Cut in butter, add sugar and knead till dough is smooth. Cut into three

[137]

equal parts, roll to fit and place in three floured cake pans. Bake for thirty minutes in a slow oven (300 degrees F.). Cool layers and remove carefully from pans. Spread jam between layers and sprinkle top with confectioners' sugar. Yield: ten or more servings.

BUTTER TORTE II

1¼ cup sweet butter	2 cups sifted flour
⅓ cup sugar	1 teaspoon baking powder
8 eggs, separated	1 teaspoon vanilla
	½ cup jam or preserves

Cream butter well, add sugar and, one by one, the egg yolks, mixing continuously for twenty minutes by hand or in electric mixer till thick. Beat egg whites until stiff and fold into mixture. Sift together flour and baking powder, blend into batter and add vanilla.

Bake in two floured layer-cake pans for about thirty-five minutes or until brown, in a moderate oven (350 degrees F.). Cool and spread jam between and on top. Then cover whole torte with Vanilla Icing, using a hot knife. Yield: twelve or more servings.

Tortes

Vanilla Icing

2 cups sifted confec-
tioners' sugar
¼ cup light cream

2 teaspoons vanilla
1 teaspoon sweet butter

Mix sugar and cream, stirring until smooth. Add vanilla and butter. If icing is too thin add more sugar; if too thick add a little more cream.

CHAUDEAU TORTE

½ cup sugar
6 eggs
4 egg yolks
1 teaspoon cornstarch
6 tablespoons sweet
butter, melted

⅔ cup sifted flour
½ teaspoon baking
powder
⅓ cup jam
½ cup heavy cream,
whipped, optional

Place sugar, eggs, egg yolks and cornstarch in a double boiler and cook, beating continuously, until mixture thickens. Remove from heat and add cooled melted butter. Sift together flour and baking powder and blend into custard. Pour batter into a buttered spring-form and bake in a slow oven (300 degrees F.) about forty-five minutes or until done. Cool, split cake into two layers and spread jam between. Cover torte with whipped cream, if desired. Yield: ten to twelve servings.

CHERRY TORTE

1 cup sugar

10 eggs, separated

½ teaspoon cinnamon

3 ounces ground sweet chocolate

1¾ cups almonds, ground

1 scant cup sifted flour

1 teaspoon baking powder

1 pound fresh cherries, pitted

Mix sugar, egg yolks and cinnamon for twenty-five minutes by hand or in electric mixer till thick. Blend in chocolate and add almonds gradually. Beat egg whites stiffly and fold in. Sift together flour and baking powder and add to mixture. Pour into a deep buttered and floured nine-inch cake form and top with cherries, which will sink into the batter. Bake in a slow oven (325 degrees F.) about one hour. Serve the following day. Yield: twelve or more servings.

CHESTNUT TORTE I

~~~~~~~~~~~~~~~~~~~~~~~~~~~~~~~~~~~~~

1 pound chestnuts,   1 teaspoon vanilla
   boiled (page 92)   4 eggs, separated
1 cup sugar   ½ cup almonds, ground

Remove skins from chestnuts and pass through a sieve or grinder, or mash well. Blend two-thirds of purée with sugar and vanilla. Reserve remainder for filling. Add egg yolks, one by one, and mix for thirty minutes by hand or in electric mixer till thick. Add almonds and fold in stiffly beaten egg whites. Pour mixture into a buttered spring form or two layer pans and bake in a slow oven (325 degrees F.) about forty-five minutes. Cool completely, split and spread Mocha Filling between layers and over top and sides of torte. Yield: twelve servings.

Mocha Filling

~~~~~~~~~~~~~~~~~~~~~~~~~~~~~~~~~~~~~

½ cup sweet   4 tablespoons very strong
   butter   coffee
½ cup sugar   2 tablespoons ground sweet
2 egg yolks   chocolate

Cream butter with sugar and add egg yolks. Mix in cold coffee, chocolate and the reserved chestnuts.

CHESTNUT TORTE II

1 cup sweet butter
1½ cups sugar
15 egg yolks
10 ounces chestnuts,
    boiled (page 92)

½ teaspoon powdered
    coffee
11 egg whites
2 tablespoons shaved
    almonds

Cream butter and sugar by hand or use electric mixer. Add egg yolks, one by one, and cream well. Pass chestnuts through a sieve or grinder and add to creamed mixture. Stir in coffee and lastly fold in stiffly beaten egg whites. Bake in layers in two well-buttered spring forms for about forty minutes in a slow oven (325 degrees F.). Remove spring-form rings, let cool, spread Chestnut Rum Filling between layers, leaving one layer on bottom of spring form. Cover torte with meringue made by beating four additional egg whites with three-fourths cup sugar till mixture forms peaks. Sprinkle with shaved almonds and return torte to oven for about ten minutes or until meringue is lightly browned. Yield: twelve or more servings.

Chestnut Rum Filling

4 tablespoons boiled
sieved chestnuts

⅓ cup sugar

2 egg whites

2 tablespoons rum

Mix all ingredients until well blended.

CHESTNUT TORTE III

5 egg whites   1⅛ cups filberts, ground

Beat egg whites stiffly and mix filberts in lightly. Line two layer pans with buttered waxed paper. Pour equal parts of batter into each pan and bake in a slow oven (325 degrees F.) fifteen to twenty minutes or until light brown. Cool, remove carefully and spread filling between layers, then cover with chocolate icing (page 132). Yield: ten or more servings.

Chestnut Cream Filling

1 pound chestnuts,
boiled (page 92)

4 tablespoons sweet
butter

½ cup sugar

2 tablespoons heavy
cream, whipped

Pass chestnuts through a sieve or grinder. Add creamed butter, sugar and whipped cream and mix thoroughly.

CHOCOLATE TORTE

1 cup sugar	2 tablespoons ground
9 eggs, separated	chocolate
1 cup walnuts, ground	2 tablespoons rum
1 tablespoon cracker meal	

Cream sugar and egg yolks well. Add walnuts and then cracker meal, chocolate and rum. Fold in stiffly beaten egg whites and pour into a deep buttered cake form. Bake in a moderate oven (350 degrees F.) about thirty minutes. After cake has cooled, preferably the next day, split and spread the following filling between layers and over top of cake. Yield: twelve or more servings.

Rum Filling

4 egg yolks	5 ounces sweet chocolate,
⅔ cup sugar	melted
⅔ cup sweet butter	1 teaspoon rum

Cream egg yolks with sugar, add butter slowly, creaming continuously. Blend in chocolate slowly and then add the rum. Chill in refrigerator for about thirty minutes before spreading.

CHOCOLATE TORTE WITH ALMONDS I

⅔ cup sweet butter
5 squares sweet chocolate, melted
¾ cup sugar

3 eggs, separated
½ cup almonds, ground
⅔ cup sifted flour

Cream butter and add slowly while mixing, chocolate, sugar and egg yolks. Mix for fifteen minutes by hand or in electric mixer till thick. Add almonds and mix fifteen minutes longer. Beat egg whites until stiff and fold into mixture. Blend the flour in lightly. Pour into a deep buttered and floured cake form and bake in a slow oven (325 degrees F.) about forty-five minutes. Cool on a cake rack and cover with Chocolate Icing (page 132). Yield: ten or more servings.

CHOCOLATE TORTE WITH ALMONDS II

1⅓ cups sugar
16 egg yolks
1⅛ cups almonds, ground

1¾ cups ground sweet chocolate
12 egg whites
1 cup sifted flour

Cream sugar and egg yolks fifteen minutes by hand or in electric mixer till thick. Mix in almonds and chocolate. Fold in stiffly beaten egg whites. Blend in flour lightly. Pour into a deep buttered and floured spring form and bake in a moderate oven (350 degrees F.) one hour. Remove ring, cool and cover with any desired icing. Yield: sixteen or more servings.

COFFEE CRÈME TORTE

7 egg whites
½ cup blanched almonds, ground

¾ cup sugar
⅓ cup finely chopped almonds

Beat egg whites stiffly and fold in the ground almonds, which have been mixed with sugar. Line three layer pans with buttered waxed paper and pour equal amounts of mixture into each. Bake in a slow oven (300 degrees F.) fifteen minutes. Remove carefully when cooled and spread Coffee Crème between layers and over top and sides. Sprinkle top and sides with chopped almonds. Yield: ten to twelve servings.

Tortes

Coffee Crème

4 egg yolks
¾ cup sugar
½ teaspoon corn-
   starch

¼ cup very strong coffee
¾ cup sweet butter,
   creamed

Cream egg yolks with sugar in a double boiler. Add cornstarch and coffee and cook, stirring continuously, until thickened. Remove from heat and continue stirring until cooled. Add slowly to the creamed butter and mix until crème is smooth.

DATE TORTE

6 egg whites
3 cups walnuts, chopped
10 ounces dates, diced
1 cup sugar

½ pint heavy cream
1 tablespoon cocoa
2 tablespoons ground
   walnuts

Beat whites of eggs stiffly. Add walnuts and dates and then blend in the sugar. Pour into a deep buttered cake form and bake in a moderately hot oven (375 degrees F.) about thirty minutes. Cool. Whip cream, blend in cocoa and cover the cake. Sprinkle top with ground walnuts. Yield: twelve or more servings.

TORTE À LA BUDAPEST I
DOBOS TORTE

Prepare and bake a Chaudeau Torte (page 139). Cool thoroughly, slice into six thin layers (preferably the next day), and fill with Chocolate Filling. Frost top of cake with Burnt Sugar Icing. Work quickly before frosting hardens. It is also desirable to cut through frosting so as to mark the servings while frosting is soft. Yield: twelve or more servings.

Chocolate Filling

1 cup sweet butter, creamed
7 ounces sweet chocolate, melted
½ teaspoon cinnamon

Blend butter and chocolate. Add cinnamon and stir until mixture is smooth.

Burned Sugar Icing

Heat half a cup of sugar in a heavy saucepan over low heat, stirring continuously, until sugar turns light brown. Pour immediately on top of torte and spread evenly with a hot knife.

TORTE À LA BUDAPEST II
DOBOS TORTE

½ cup plus one tablespoon sugar	½ cup plus one tablespoon sifted flour
9 eggs, separated	½ teaspoon baking powder

Cream sugar and egg yolks well. Sift together flour and baking powder and blend in thoroughly. Beat egg whites stiffly and fold in. Bake six separate layers in buttered layer pans or cake forms in a moderate oven (350 degrees F.) about five minutes or until light brown. Cool thoroughly. Fill and frost as Torte à la Budapest I (page 148). Yield: twelve or more servings.

TORTE ELEGANTE

½ cup sultana raisins	1¾ cups milk
6 tablespoons rum	2 envelopes unflavored gelatin
1 recipe Macaroon Torte (page 166)	½ cup warm water
1 cup sugar	½ pint heavy cream, whipped
9 egg yolks	½ cup shredded almonds
1 teaspoon cornstarch	
1 teaspoon vanilla	

Soak sultanas in half the rum overnight. Prepare Macaroon Torte and bake in one cake form instead of three. Cool, split into three layers and fill with the following crème:

Cream sugar and egg yolks in a double boiler, add cornstarch, vanilla and milk. Cook, stirring until mixture has thickened. Remove from heat. Soften gelatin in warm water, add to crème and stir till dissolved. Cool and add remaining rum. Fold in whipped cream.

Place one layer of torte in a cake form which is one inch larger in diameter than the torte. Pour a one-half inch layer of crème over cake and around torte layer. Chill till firm. Place second layer on top, sprinkle with half the sultanas and cover again with one-half inch of crème. Refrigerate till firm. Place third layer on top, sprinkle with last of sultanas, cover with last of crème and return to refrigerator. When completely chilled, turn torte onto a cake plate and dress top and sides with almonds by sticking them in like quills. Yield: twelve or more servings.

EMPEROR TORTE

¾ cup sweet butter
¾ cup sugar
4 ounces sweet chocolate
7 eggs, separated

1 cup almonds, ground
½ teaspoon baking powder
¼ cup finely chopped almonds

Cream butter and sugar. Melt chocolate in a double boiler, add and blend in slowly. Add egg yolks gradually, then ground almonds and baking powder. Fold in stiffly beaten egg whites. Bake in two greased layer pans about thirty minutes in a moderate oven (350 degrees F.). Cool thoroughly. Spread Chocolate Nut Filling between layers and over top of torte. Sprinkle with chopped almonds. Yield: twelve or more servings.

Chocolate Nut Filling

4 eggs
¼ cup sugar
½ teaspoon cornstarch
½ cup butter, creamed

3½ ounces sweet chocolate, melted
½ cup walnuts, ground
1 teaspoon vanilla

Break eggs into a double boiler, add sugar and cornstarch and cook, stirring, until just thickened. Cool mixture, add butter, chocolate, nuts, vanilla; blend well.

ELVIRA TORTE

2½ cups walnuts, ground   ⅓ cup cracker meal
1⅔ cups almonds, ground   ¼ cup heavy cream,
1¼ cups sugar   whipped
½ teaspoon powdered   10 eggs
    coffee

Mix walnuts, almonds, sugar and coffee. To one-half cup of this mixture add cracker meal. Reserve remainder. Place cream in saucepan and bring to a boil, add nuts and cracker meal mixture, stir and cook until thick, remove from heat and let cool.

To the reserved nut mixture, add gradually six egg yolks and four whole eggs, then fold in the six egg whites, beaten stiffly. Pour into two layer pans, which have been buttered and floured, and bake in a slow oven (325 degrees F.) about thirty minutes. Cool on a cake rack and spread the cooked mixture between the layers. Cover with Chocolate Icing (page 132). Yield: twelve or more servings.

FILBERT TORTE I

1⅓ cups sugar
12 egg yolks
2 cups filberts, ground
½ teaspoon powdered
coffee

3 tablespoons ground
sweet chocolate
8 egg whites

Cream sugar and egg yolks thirty minutes by hand or in electric mixer till thick. Add filberts, coffee and chocolate. Beat egg whites stiffly and fold in. Pour into two buttered and floured layer pans and bake in a slow oven (325 degrees F.) about forty-five minutes. When cool, spread Filbert Filling between layers, cover with Maraschino Icing and dress with glazed cherries. Yield: twelve or more servings.

Filbert Filling

2 egg whites
⅓ cup sugar
3 tablespoons ground sweet
chocolate

1 tablespoon finely
chopped filberts

Beat egg whites stiffly, add sugar gradually and fold in rest of ingredients.

[**153**]

Maraschino Icing

2 cups confectioners' sugar
2 tablespoons maraschino syrup

1 teaspoon sweet butter, or
1 tablespoon light cream

Mix sugar and maraschino syrup until smooth. Add butter or cream, and if icing is too thick, add a little more cream or milk.

FILBERT TORTE II

Prepare Filbert Torte I (page 153) and cool thoroughly. Make a filling of one-half cup heavy cream, whipped, and mixed with one tablespoon sugar. Cover torte with the following Meringue. Yield: twelve or more servings.

Meringue

4 egg whites
¾ cup sugar

1 teaspoon vanilla

Beat egg whites stiffly, add sugar and vanilla. Cut waxed paper the same size and shape as top of torte, butter paper, place on a cookie sheet and cover paper with meringue. Bake in a slow oven (350 degrees F.)

about five minutes. Remove meringue carefully from paper, using a thin knife, and transfer to top of torte.

FRUIT TORTE I

¾ cup sweet butter
1⅓ cups sifted flour
½ cup almonds
⅓ cup sugar
½ teaspoon cinnamon

½ cup jam or preserves
1 tablespoon powdered
  sugar
½ pint heavy cream,
  whipped

Cut butter into flour, add and knead in ground almonds, sugar and cinnamon, kneading until dough is smooth. Cut dough into three equal parts, roll each and fit it into a floured layer pan or spring form. Bake layers about twenty minutes in a moderate oven (350 degrees F.). Cool, and remove very carefully from pans. Spread jam or preserves between layers and over top. Sprinkle top with powdered sugar or spread with whipped cream. Yield: ten or more servings.

GRAPE TORTE

Prepare torte layers as for Fruit Torte I. Spread currant jelly between layers, cover top with fresh seeded grapes and garnish with whipped cream.

RASPBERRY TORTE

Prepare torte layers as for Fruit Torte I. Spread raspberry jam between layers. Cover top with fresh or frozen raspberries and whipped cream.

STRAWBERRY TORTE

Bake and cool three layers of Fruit Torte I. Spread strawberry jam between layers, cover top thickly with hulled fresh strawberries and garnish with whipped cream.

FRUIT TORTE II

$2/3$ cup sweet butter
1 cup plus three tablespoons sifted flour
1 tablespoon white vinegar
2 tablespoons sour cream
2 pounds fresh apricots, halved

2 tablespoons cracker meal
2 tablespoons sugar
3 egg whites
3 tablespoons confectioners' sugar
$1/3$ cup finely diced or chopped almonds

Cut butter into flour, add vinegar and sour cream and knead well. If too sticky add a little more flour. Cover and place in refrigerator for one-half hour. Roll dough on a floured board to fit into a deep buttered spring form. Bake for thirty minutes in a hot oven (400 degrees F.). At this stage the torte is only partly baked. Mix apricots with cracker meal, cover torte with mixture and sprinkle with the two tablespoons sugar. Return to oven and bake for twenty minutes more.

Remove from oven again and cover with meringue made by beating egg whites with confectioners' sugar. Sprinkle with almonds. Reduce temperature to low (300 degrees F.) and bake ten minutes longer. Cool before removing from pan. Yield: twelve or more servings.

Note: Other fresh fruits may be substituted for apricots.

GIZELLE TORTE

1½ cups filberts, ground
6 egg whites

2 cups sifted confectioners' sugar

Mix filberts with egg whites. Add sugar and blend well. Line two layer pans with buttered waxed paper, spread equal amounts of paste in each and bake in a moderate oven (350 degrees F.) about fifteen minutes. Remove carefully after cooling, spread Apricot Crème between layers. Then cover torte with Vanilla Icing (page 139) or Lemon Icing (page 54). Yield: about ten servings.

Apricot Crème Filling

4 egg whites   ⅓ cup warm apricot jam
¾ cup sugar

Beat egg whites until stiff, mix in sugar lightly and add jam.

GRILLAGE TORTE

9 egg whites   ½ teaspoon baking powder
1½ cups sugar   ½ teaspoon almond extract
1½ cups almonds,
    ground

Beat egg whites, add sugar and beat until stiff. Fold in almonds, stir in baking powder and almond extract. Bake in a buttered 5 x 9-inch loaf pan or a deep eight-inch layer cake form for about forty-five minutes in a moderate oven (350 degrees F.). Cool, preferably over-night, cut into two layers. Spread the following filling between layers and on top and sides. Sprinkle with grillage. Yield: twelve or more servings.

Tortes

Coffee Filling

~~~~~~

½ cup plus one tablespoon
   sugar

9 egg yolks

3 tablespoons very strong
   coffee

2 tablespoons sifted
   flour

1 teaspoon cornstarch

½ teaspoon vanilla

⅔ cup sweet butter

Mix sugar and egg yolks in a double boiler until smooth. Add gradually rest of ingredients except the butter. Cook over low heat, stirring until mixture thickens. Let it cool, then blend in creamed butter.

Grillage

~~~~~~

½ cup sugar

1 cup broken walnuts

Heat sugar in a heavy saucepan over low heat, stirring continuously until melted. Add walnuts and stir until sugar and walnuts have turned light brown. Pour mixture *quickly* on a very wet board trying, with a spoon, to keep mixture as nearly as possible in a lump. Let cool until hardened, at least two hours, and chop into very small pieces, using a hammer.

[159]

TORTE À LA HELLER

⅔ cup almonds,
   ground
7 eggs
4 egg yolks

¾ cup sugar
¾ cup flour
½ teaspoon baking
   powder

Place almonds in a double boiler and mix in eggs one by one. Gradually add egg yolks and sugar. Cook, beating continuously, until mixture thickens. Remove from heat and continue beating until mixture has cooled. Sift flour and baking powder together and blend in lightly. Pour into a deep buttered and floured cake form and bake in a slow oven (325 degrees F.) about forty-five minutes. Cool and ice as desired. Garnish with candied fruits or nuts. Yield: ten or more servings.

TORTE HOLLANDAISE

1¼ cups sweet butter
⅔ cup sugar
1 tablespoon lemon juice
½ teaspoon cinnamon

3 cups sifted flour
1 teaspoon baking
   powder
½ cup jam

Cream butter, add sugar, lemon juice and cinnamon and mix thoroughly. Sift together flour and baking

[**160**]

powder, add and knead dough on a floured board until smooth. Divide into three parts, roll to fit and place in three layer pans which have been lined with buttered waxed paper. Bake in a moderate oven (350 degrees F.) about thirty minutes. Cool and spread jam between layers. Yield: twelve or more servings.

IMPERIAL TORTE

1⅔ cups sugar

10 eggs, separated

⅔ cup sifted flour

1⅓ cups sweet butter

2 cups almonds, ground

1½ cups jam

Place sugar in mixing bowl, adding alternately one egg yolk and one tablespoon flour and mixing well after each addition. Continue mixing for thirty minutes by hand or in electric mixer till thick. Melt butter and add almonds gradually, alternating a little melted butter with a little of the almonds. Beat egg whites until stiff and fold in. Pour into three layer pans which have been buttered and floured. Bake in a slow oven (300 degrees F.) about forty-five minutes. Cool and spread jam between layers. Cover with Vanilla Icing (page 139) or Lemon Icing (page 54). Yield: twelve or more servings.

[**161**]

TORTE ITALIENNE I

1⅓ cups sugar
12 eggs, separated
1¾ cups sifted flour
1 teaspoon baking
powder

1 teaspoon vanilla
1 recipe Chocolate Icing
(page 132)
2 squares sweet chocolate

Blend sugar and egg yolks, adding them one by one, and mix about twenty minutes by hand or in electric beater till thick. Beat egg whites until stiff and fold into mixture. Sift together flour and baking powder, blend in and add vanilla. Bake in a buttered spring form about one hour in a slow oven (300 degrees F.). Cool torte, cut into three layers and spread the following filling between layers. Cover with Chocolate Icing, using six ounces of chocolate instead of four. Yield: twelve or more servings.

Chocolate Filling

3 egg whites
½ cup powdered sugar

4 ounces ground sweet
chocolate

Beat egg whites stiffly, add sugar, beat till stiff and blend in chocolate.

Tortes

¾ cup plus two table-
   spoons sweet butter
⅓ cup sugar
6 eggs, separated
2 cups sifted flour
1 teaspoon baking
   powder

1 teaspoon vanilla
1 recipe Chocolate
   Filling (above), or
    ½ cup jam or jelly
1 recipe Chocolate Icing
   (page 132)

Cream butter, add sugar and mix fifteen minutes by hand or in electric mixer. Add egg yolks gradually and continue mixing ten minutes. Beat egg whites stiffly and fold into mixture. Sift flour with baking powder, fold into batter, and add vanilla. Bake in a buttered spring form about one hour in a slow oven (300 degrees F.). Cool, cut into three layers, spread with Chocolate Filling or jam and frost with Chocolate Icing. Yield: ten servings.

LILY TORTE

6 eggs, separated

6 tablespoons sugar

2 heaping tablespoons
cocoa or ground
chocolate

3 tablespoons sifted
flour

½ teaspoon baking
powder

½ teaspoon vanilla

Cream egg yolks and sugar till light and fluffy and add cocoa or chocolate. Beat egg whites stiffly and fold in. Add flour and baking powder which have been sifted together and add vanilla. Bake in two greased layer pans for about thirty minutes in a moderate oven (350 degrees F.). Cool, spread Walnut Butter Filling between layers and cover with Lemon Icing (page 54) or Cherry Icing made by substituting two tablespoons maraschino cherry syrup and three tablespoons milk for the lemon juice. Yield: eight to ten servings.

Walnut Butter Filling

⅓ cup hot milk

1 cup walnuts, ground

6 tablespoons sugar

6 tablespoons sweet
butter, creamed

Pour hot milk over ground walnuts. Add sugar and butter and blend.

Tortes

LINZER TORTE I

~~~~~~

1 cup almonds, ground

1 egg white

1⅓ cups sweet butter, creamed

1¼ cups sugar

6 egg yolks

1 teaspoon vanilla

2⅓ cups sifted flour

1 teaspoon baking powder

2 tablespoons powdered sugar

Mix almonds with egg white. Add gradually creamed butter, sugar, egg yolks and vanilla and mix for fifteen minutes by hand or in electric mixer till thick. Sift together flour and baking powder and blend in. Pour mixture into a deep buttered and floured cake form and bake in a moderate oven (350 degrees F.) about forty-five minutes. When cooled dust with powdered sugar. Yield: ten or more servings.

LINZER TORTE II

~~~~~~

1⅓ cups sweet butter

1⅔ cups sugar

2⅓ cups blanched almonds, ground

2 tablespoons lemon juice

1 teaspoon vanilla

8 eggs, separated

2⅓ cups sifted flour

1 teaspoon baking powder

Cream butter with sugar, add almonds, lemon juice, vanilla and, gradually, the egg yolks. Mix for fifteen minutes by hand or in electric mixer till thick. Fold in stiffly beaten whites of eggs, blend in lightly flour which has been sifted with baking powder. Butter and flour a deep cake form, pour in batter and bake about one hour in a moderate oven (350 degrees F.). Yield: sixteen or more servings.

MACAROON TORTE

6 egg whites	1 teaspoon baking
1¼ cups sugar	powder
1⅔ cups almonds,	1 teaspoon vanilla
ground	

Beat egg whites stiffly, add sugar and continue beating until well blended. Mix almonds and baking powder and add to mixture. Lastly add vanilla. Bake in two greased layer pans for about thirty minutes in a moderate oven (350 degrees F.). When thoroughly cooled, preferably next day, fill cake and cover with following Coffee Frosting. Yield: ten or more servings.

Coffee Frosting

~~~~~~~~~~~~~~~~~~~~~~~~~~~

3 egg yolks　　　　　½ teaspoon cornstarch
½ cup sugar　　　　　¾ cup sweet butter
¾ cup cold strong
　　coffee

Cream yolks and sugar in a double boiler. Mix in gradually coffee and cornstarch. Cook, stirring occasionally, until mixture thickens. Cool completely. Cream butter and blend into mixture until smooth.

NUT TORTE I

~~~~~~~~~~~~~~~~~~~~~~~~~~~

7 eggs, separated　　　⅔ cup flour
¼ cup sugar　　　　　½ teaspoon baking
½ cup broken walnuts,　　　powder
　　ground
10 graham crackers,
　　crushed

Cream egg yolks with sugar, add walnuts and graham crackers. Beat egg whites stiffly, fold into mixture, then mix in gradually flour which has been sifted with baking powder. Bake in a deep buttered and floured cake form for about forty-five minutes in a slow oven (300 degrees F.). Cool torte and if desired, cover with whipped cream. Yield: ten or more servings.

NUT TORTE II

1¼ cups sweet butter
1⅓ cups sugar
6 egg yolks
2½ cups walnuts, ground

1 egg white
2 cups sifted flour
1 teaspoon baking powder

Cream butter, sugar and egg yolks for about fifteen minutes by hand or in electric mixer till thick. Add walnuts with the egg white. Continue mixing for about ten minutes. Sift together flour and baking powder and blend in. Bake in a deep buttered and floured spring form for about one hour in a slow oven (300 degrees F.). Cool torte and cover with Chocolate Topping. Yield: twelve or more servings.

Chocolate Topping

Melt four ounces of semi-sweet chocolate in a double boiler and spread over torte.

Tortes

ORANGE TORTE I

2/3 cup sweet butter
1¼ cups sugar
1 orange
8 hard-cooked egg
  yolks

8 raw egg yolks
4 egg whites
2/3 cup sifted flour
½ teaspoon baking
  powder

Cream butter, add sugar, grated rind and juice of orange and mix for twenty minutes by hand or in electric mixer. Sieve the hard-cooked egg yolks, add to mixture together with the raw egg yolks and continue mixing for about ten more minutes. Beat egg whites stiffly and fold in. Add flour which has been sifted with baking powder. Bake in a 9-inch spring form, which has been buttered and sprinkled with flour, for about one hour in a slow oven (300 degrees F.). Cool and frost with Orange Icing (page 136). Yield: twelve or more servings.

ORANGE TORTE II

1¼ cups sugar
12 egg yolks
2 cups blanched almonds,
  ground

1 teaspoon baking
  powder
1 orange
6 egg whites

[169]

Mix sugar with egg yolks for about twenty minutes by hand or in electric mixer till thick. Mix almonds with baking powder and blend into mixture. Add grated orange rind and juice. Continue mixing for ten minutes more. Beat egg whites stiffly and fold in lightly. Bake in a deep greased and floured spring form in a slow oven (300 degrees F.) about one hour. Cool and frost with Orange Icing (page 136). Yield: twelve or more servings.

SACHER TORTE I

¾ cup sweet butter
¾ cup sugar
5½ ounces sweet
　chocolate
6 eggs, separated
1 teaspoon almond
　extract

1¼ cups sifted flour
1 teaspoon baking powder
½ cup jam
½ pint heavy cream,
　whipped.

Cream butter with sugar well. Melt chocolate in double boiler, add and blend in slowly. Add the egg yolks one by one. Beat egg whites stiffly, fold in and add almond extract. Sift together flour and baking powder and blend in lightly. Bake in two buttered layer pans about thirty minutes in a moderate oven (350 degrees F.).

Cool, spread jam between layers and cover with whipped cream. The whipped cream for this torte can be made especially delicious by adding one tablespoon ground sweet chocolate and one tablespoon confectioners' sugar. Yield: ten or more servings.

SACHER TORTE II

¾ cup sweet butter	4 tablespoons flour
6 tablespoons sugar	½ teaspoon baking
4 eggs, separated	powder
3½ ounces semisweet	½ cup jam
chocolate, melted	½ pint heavy cream,
¾ cup almonds	whipped

Cream butter and sugar well. Add gradually egg yolks, chocolate, ground almonds and flour which has been sifted with baking powder. Lastly fold in stiffly beaten egg whites. Bake in two buttered layer pans about thirty minutes in a moderate oven (350 degrees F.). After cooling spread jam between layers and cover with whipped cream. The whipped cream for this torte can be made especially delicious by adding one tablespoon of ground sweet chocolate and one tablespoon of confectioners' sugar. Yield: ten or more servings.

SAND TORTE I

~~~~~~

1¼ cups sweet   Juice and rind of one
    butter   lemon
1⅓ cups sugar   2 cups sifted flour
8 eggs, separated   1 teaspoon baking powder

Cream butter with sugar, add egg yolks gradually, stir in lemon juice and grated rind and mix for thirty minutes by hand or in electric mixer. Beat egg whites stiffly and fold in. Sift flour with baking powder and blend in lightly. Pour mixture into a deep buttered and floured cake form and bake in a slow oven (325 degrees F.) about one hour. After torte has cooled cover with any desired icing. Yield: ten or more servings.

SAND TORTE II

~~~~~~

6 egg whites   ½ cup rice meal
¾ cup sugar   ¼ cup flour
8 egg yolks   3 tablespoons sweet butter

Beat egg whites stiffly, add sugar, egg yolks gradually and then blend in lightly rice meal and flour which have been sifted together. Melt butter, let it cool and add carefully to avoid curdling. When all ingredients have been blended, pour into a deep buttered and floured cake form and bake in a moderate oven (350 degrees F.) about forty-five minutes. After torte has cooled cover with Lemon or Orange Icing (page 136). Yield: ten or more servings.

SNOW TORTE

10 egg whites
1⅔ cups sugar
2⅓ cups almonds, ground

⅓ cup candied lemon rind, chopped finely

Beat whites of eggs stiffly and add sugar. Fold in almonds and lemon rind. Bake in a deep well-buttered cake form for a little over one hour in a slow oven (300 degrees F.). Serve the following day. Yield: twelve or more servings.

SUGAR TORTE À LA FRANÇAISE

2 cups sweet butter
¾ cup sugar
8 egg yolks

4½ cups flour
1 teaspoon baking powder
¾ cup jam or jelly

Cream butter with sugar, add egg yolks gradually and continue creaming for fifteen minutes by hand or in electric mixer till thick. Sift flour with baking powder, add to mixture and knead dough until smooth. Cover and refrigerate for thirty minutes. Place on a floured board and cut into three equal parts. Roll each part to about one-half-inch thickness and fit into three greased and floured cake pans. Bake layers about one hour in a slow oven (300 degrees F.). Cool completely, spread jam or jelly between layers and cover with Lemon Icing (page 136). Yield: sixteen or more servings.

TORTE NAPOLEON

3/4 cup sweet butter
3/4 cup sugar
4 eggs, separated
1 cup almonds, ground
6 ounces ground sweet chocolate
Grated rind of one-half lemon
Grated rind of one-half orange
1/2 teaspoon cinnamon
1/2 teaspoon almond extract
2/3 cup sifted flour
1 teaspoon baking powder
1/2 cup jam
Lemon Icing (page 136)

Cream butter, add sugar gradually and add the egg yolks, one by one. Mix about twenty minutes by hand or in electric mixer till thick. Blend almonds in slowly. Add chocolate, lemon and orange rinds, cinnamon and almond extract. Beat egg whites stiffly and fold in. Sift flour and baking powder together and add.

Turn into three greased and floured cake forms or layer pans. Bake in a slow oven (300 degrees F.) thirty-five to forty minutes. Cool torte completely and spread any kind of jam between layers. Cover with Lemon Icing. Yield: ten or more servings.

TRIESTE TORTE

1¼ cups sweet butter
1⅓ cups sugar
16 egg yolks
1 cup almonds, ground
½ teaspoon baking powder

2 cups crushed zwieback
4 egg whites
1 tablespoon confectioners' sugar

Cream butter and sugar, add egg yolks gradually, and add almonds which have been mixed with baking powder and crushed zwieback. Beat egg whites stiffly and fold into mixture. Pour into a deep well-buttered and floured cake form, and bake about forty-five minutes in a slow oven (300 degrees F.). Cool and sprinkle with confectioners' sugar or cover with any preferred icing. Yield: ten or more servings.

VIENNESE ALMOND TORTE

Mixture I

8 egg yolks	1 teaspoon baking powder
1¼ cups sugar	4 egg whites
1¾ cups almonds, ground	½ lemon

Cream egg yolks with sugar until smooth and fluffy. Mix almonds and baking powder and blend into mixture. Beat egg whites stiffly, fold in and add grated lemon rind and juice. Bake in a large buttered layer-cake pan or spring form about thirty minutes in a moderate oven (350 degrees F.).

Mixture II

8 egg whites	1 teaspoon baking powder
1¼ cups sugar	½ lemon
1¾ cups blanched almonds, ground	

Beat egg whites until stiff, add sugar gradually while beating. Mix almond and baking powder, blend into meringue and add grated rind and lemon juice. Turn into a buttered spring form, of the same size as that used for Mixture I, and bake in a moderate oven (350 degrees F.) thirty-five to forty minutes. Cool torte thoroughly. Spread the following frosting between mixtures I and II and over top and sides. Yield: twelve or more servings.

Almond Frosting

4 egg yolks	$\frac{1}{2}$ teaspoon cornstarch
4 tablespoons sugar	$\frac{1}{2}$ cup sweet butter
$\frac{1}{4}$ cup strong coffee	Ground almonds, optional
$\frac{1}{4}$ cup sifted flour	

Cream egg yolks and sugar well in a double boiler. Blend in coffee. Combine flour with cornstarch and add. Cook, stirring, until thickened. Cool thoroughly and add the creamed butter. Sprinkle ground almonds on top of torte.

~~~~~~

6 eggs, separated
¾ cup sugar
1½ cups walnuts, ground
½ teaspoon baking powder

1 tablespoon powdered coffee
2 tablespoons jam
½ pint heavy cream, whipped

Beat egg whites until stiff, add sugar and mix well. Blend in yolks one at a time. Mix walnuts and baking powder, add to mixture and add coffee. Pour into a deep buttered cake form and bake in a moderate oven (350 degrees F.) about thirty minutes. Cool, spread jam on top of cake and cover with whipped cream. Yield: ten to twelve servings.

INDEX

~~~~~~~~~~

Index

Index

Index

Index

Index

Index

Index